Faith Stronger Than Bullets is a raw, redemptive testimony of what it looks like to cling to God when life's world collapses. Kashe's story is more than perseverance—it is an invitation to encounter Jesus in the pain, the questions, and the slow unfolding of hope. Through vivid honesty and unwavering faith, she demonstrates that while suffering may shape us, it never defines us. This book will comfort the brokenhearted, encourage the weary, and point every reader toward the God who sustains us not in spite of our storms, but through them.

—**Jenny Leavitt, Author of** *GodPrints: Finding Evidence of God in the Shattered Pieces of Life,* **Founder of GodPrints Ministry, Grief recovery advocate, Creator of the Resilient Grief Recovery Courses, BCMMHC Specializing in Grief Loss Trauma-informed Care, www.jennyleavitt.com, www.resilienthope.net**

PRAISE FOR:
Faith Stronger Than Bullets

Faith Stronger Than Bullets is a powerful testimony of resilience, faith, and divine preservation. Kashe writes with raw honesty and spiritual depth, inviting readers into the painful realities of loss, trauma, and survival—while never losing sight of God's sustaining grace. This memoir does more than tell a story; it ministers. As the author of *You Don't Know Just How I Feel*, and as a professor, paralegal, and doctoral student who has spent years studying grief, justice, and human experience, I recognize the rare courage it takes to tell the truth this openly. Kashe's story speaks to those who have been wounded by violence and to those who walk beside them, offering hope without minimizing pain. This book reminds us that faith does not eliminate suffering—but it strengthens us to endure, heal, and rise. *Faith Stronger Than Bullets* is a necessary and timely work that will resonate deeply with readers seeking understanding, encouragement, and the assurance that God's presence remains even in our darkest moments.

—Gwendolyn Burton, Author of *You Don't Know Just How I Feel*, Professor, Paralegal, Doctoral Student

As a counselor, life coach, retired Chief Warrant Officer 4 in the United States Army, and ordained minister, I have accompanied many individuals and families through the devastating loss of loved ones. I recognize the long-term emotional and spiritual impact these experiences leave behind. This book acknowledges that trauma is real and that grief does not follow a linear path—yet it also affirms that God's presence remains steadfast throughout the journey. *Faith Stronger Than Bullets* is a deeply moving and necessary testimony that speaks to the reality of grief caused by sudden and senseless violence. Kashe writes with honesty, courage, and spiritual clarity, offering readers a place to sit with their pain while being gently guided toward hope and healing Kashe does not offer simplistic answers or platitudes. Instead, she provides a compassionate testimony that validates suffering while pointing readers toward resilience, faith, and restoration. *Faith Stronger Than Bullets* will be an invaluable resource for those navigating grief, as well as for counselors, pastors, and caregivers seeking to support individuals affected by violence and loss.

—Anthony K. Hayes, Counselor, Life Coach, Retired Chief Warrant Officer 4, U.S. Army, Ordained Minister

Faith Stronger Than Bullets:

Living Proof That God Turns Pain Into Purpose

Kashe Jaranilla

All rights reserved. This book is protected by the copyright laws of the United States of America. This book may not be copied or reprinted for commercial gain or profit. The use of short quotations or occasional page copying for personal or group study is permitted and encouraged.

This book is for informational, educational, and testimonial purposes only and does not constitute professional advice. The views, experiences, and reflections expressed herein are those of the author(s) and contributors and do not necessarily reflect the views of the publisher. The publisher disclaims liability for any distress or harm arising from engagement with the content, to the extent permitted by law.

This book does not constitute, nor should it be construed as legal, medical, psychological, therapeutic, pastoral, or professional advice of any kind. Readers are advised to consult qualified professionals regarding any concerns related to physical health, mental health, trauma recovery, legal matters, or spiritual care.

This publication is intended for a general audience and is distributed internationally. Laws, professional standards, and cultural interpretations may vary by jurisdiction. The information contained herein should be interpreted in accordance with the laws and regulations applicable in the reader's place of residence.

Any personal accounts or identifying details have been included with permission or have been anonymized where appropriate. Inclusion of individual narratives does not imply endorsement of specific viewpoints, actions, or interpretations beyond the author's expressed intent.

Unless otherwise noted, Scripture quotations used in this book are from *The Holy Bible*, New International Version (NIV). © 1973, 1978, 1984, 2011 International Bible Society. Used by permission of Zondervan Bible Publishers.

Other Scripture references are from the following sources:
New King James Version (NKJV), ©1979, 1980, 1982, Thomas Nelson, Inc.
English

Copyright © 2026 Kashe Jaranilla. All rights reserved.
Faith Stronger Than Bullets: Living Proof That God Turns Pain Into Purpose, Kashe Jaranilla
Issued in electronic and paperback formats.
Paperback ISBN: 978-1-970354-10-2
E-book ISBN: 978-1-970354-11-9
LCCN: 2026903620
First Edition

Publisher: Dressed in Love Press, LLC
www.drkatherinehayes.com

Cover Designer: Katherine Hutchinson-Hayes
Book Interior Designer: Jenifer Jennings

Printed in the United States of America

This book is dedicated to the love of my life, whose life was taken far too soon, and to the two beautiful children we share. Your father's love and legacy live on through you.

To my eldest child, thank you for your strength, your patience, and the quiet courage you showed when I needed it most.

And to every survivor who has walked through unimaginable pain and chosen to keep trusting God—this story is for you. May it remind you that even in the darkest moments, God is still near, still faithful, and still at work.

"The Lord is close to the brokenhearted and saves those who are crushed in spirit."
—Psalm 34:18, NIV

Table of Contents

Content Warning i
Prologue iv
Chapter 1: My Childhood 1
Chapter 2: Paul, Also Known as Dad 7
Chapter 3: Kaniya 12
Chapter 4: Jeremiah 17
Chapter 5: Chico 22
Chapter 6: Eman 27
Chapter 7: A Warning from God 31
Chapter 8: Ambushed with Bullets 36
Chapter 9: Waking Up to My New Life 42
Chapter 10: Two Weeks Felt Like Two Decades 47
Chapter 11: Never Got to Say Goodbye & Learning to Walk Again 52
Chapter 12: Leaving Christ Hospital 57
Chapter 13: A Visit from the Other Side 63
Chapter 14: Leaving Chicago 68
Chapter 15: A Name to That Face & Digging Deeper 75
Chapter 16: Moving Again & Going Back to School 82
Chapter 17: The Start Of Many Court Dates 99
Chapter 18: Being Tested 104
Chapter 19: A Visit From An Evil Entity 110

Chapter 20: Did I Just Have Another Gun Pointed At Me?..116

Chapter 21: Go Home, Chico............................... 122

Chapter 22: The Lord Jesus Was In My Room 129

Chapter 23: Trial's Finally Here & Life After........ 136

Chapter 24: Revelation, Waking Up for Good....... 144

Chapter 25: WHY?... 150

Final Reflection: Lessons from Loss and Victory .. 158

Message to My Readers... 161

References.. 163

Faith Stronger Than Bullets: A Grief & Healing Study Guide 164

Prayer & Reflection Page...................................... 172

Leader's Guide: Walking With Others Through Grief... 173

Further Resources... 176

Acknowledgments 179

Content Warning

Some stories stop us in our tracks—not because they are easy to read, but because they reveal how suddenly life can change. They confront us with the reality that pain can arrive without warning, that justice is not guaranteed, and that healing is often a long and difficult road. Faith Stronger than Bullets is one of those stories.

Faith Stronger than Bullets speaks to a truth many know too well: life is often unfair, and the world is deeply broken. But it also declares something greater—that we serve a good God who does not abandon us in suffering. A God who draws near to the wounded. A God who transforms pain into purpose, not by erasing the past, but by redeeming it.

This book is a testimony of God's grace, restoration, and faithfulness through life's most difficult seasons. Within these pages, Kashe Jaranilla shares real experiences from her past—some of which include themes of hardship, broken relationships, and youthful decisions made without spiritual maturity.

This work includes descriptions and photographs related to gun violence and its aftermath. Such content is included solely for the purposes of documentation, education, and awareness and is not intended to sensationalize, glorify, or promote violence. Reader discretion is advised. Individual reactions to traumatic material may vary.

These moments are not presented to shock or condemn, but to bear honest witness to where God met Kashe, carried her, and began His redemptive work. All sensitive subjects are shared with discretion, prayer, and respect for readers of faith. She asks that you read her testimony with grace, remembering that growth often springs from broken places and that God's mercy meets us long before we understand His purpose. Her hope is not to glorify pain, but to magnify the faithfulness of a God who redeems every chapter of our lives.

Stories of violence and survival often awaken deep questions: Where was God in the moment of harm? How does one hold faith alongside fear, grief, or anger? What does healing look like when wounds are both visible and unseen? These questions are neither signs of weak faith nor problems to be quickly resolved. They are honest responses to suffering and deserve patience, compassion, and space.

Readers are encouraged to approach this work with gentleness toward themselves. Pausing, stepping away, or seeking counsel from a trusted pastor, counselor, or spiritual companion is an act of care. Prayer, reflection, or stillness may serve as grounding practices, but so too may practical support, professional guidance, and honest conversation.

As you read, may you be reminded that resilience is born not of human strength alone, but of surrender. And if you are carrying your own pain, may this story point you toward a God who sees you, loves you, and is ready to walk with you toward healing.

Prologue

Setting the Scene:

My eyes slowly opened, and I soon realized where I was. The hospital. It had been nearly twenty-four hours since surgery. My body felt heavy, lifeless, and my jaw was wired shut. Machines hummed, and monitors beeped steadily around me, marking time when I couldn't.

I didn't know the extent of the damage to my body or my face. All I knew was that I wanted to get up—to run—to find my children and their father. Okay, in that moment, it didn't mean comfortable or unharmed. It meant *alive*. But I couldn't move. I lay there, trapped in my own body, tears sliding silently down my face.

Fragments of memory returned. I strained recalling small details that created a big picture. Sitting in our car. The sudden chaos. Someone had been shooting at us. In an instant, everything changed. As I lay there, unable to speak or move, one question echoed louder than the beeping machines around me: *Why?*

For as long as I could remember, I believed I had been born into bad luck. Growing up, I didn't always understand the things happening around me—or to me. And now this. Lying in a hospital bed, unsure of what tomorrow would bring, I realized that this moment—this pain—was part of a story that needed to be told.

That is why I am here.

Setting the Stage:

Writing has always been my safe place. It's where my heart feels free, where I can breathe. But I knew very little about writing a book, let alone a *good* one. Still, I had to begin somewhere. For a long time, I wrestled with how to start. I wanted to remember every detail, every date, every moment perfectly. Eventually, I realized much of that was fear disguised as overthinking.

I don't remember every date. I don't remember everything. And while I never want to intentionally hurt anyone who has been part of my life, I owe it to myself—and to you—to be honest.

For years, I thought I was just an ordinary girl from the West Side of Chicago. Who would want to read about me? But as life unfolded, I came to understand that I carry a testimony—a story of devastation, yes, but also of courage. The courage to keep going, no matter the obstacles.

Today, I still wrestle with life, love, and everyday struggles. But I keep moving forward, striving to become the woman God has called me to be: educated, faithful, creative, loving, and whole. A writer. A worshiper. A wife someday. And most importantly, a phenomenal mother. I now know I cannot be any of these things without God.

I began writing this book at twenty-seven, young, hurting, and in desperate need of direction. Life had knocked me down more times than I could count. Without God and His Word, I was lost. Even now, I'm still learning Him, still growing, still becoming. Faith, I've learned, is tested the moment we declare we believe.

I used to try to read the Bible without understanding it. I felt disconnected. So, I began slowly—one verse, one prayer at a time. Building a personal relationship with God changed everything. Without Him, there is no me.

God speaks. He has spoken to me. But for a long time, I couldn't hear Him clearly because I was consumed by the world and its noise. Without Him,

I couldn't grow, love myself, or find the strength to move forward. And without that strength, how could I guide my children—three innocent lives looking to me for love, stability, and direction?

I didn't grow up with consistent guidance or stability. Love wasn't always spoken aloud. Violence, dysfunction, and survival were familiar themes. I don't share this to place blame—only to speak my truth. At some point, the cycle has to end.

I chose to be the example I didn't have. To teach my children love. To show them faith. To stop the pattern and start something new.

I once believed bad luck followed me. That stability wasn't meant for me. But I was wrong. I wasn't cursed—I was searching. And God met me right where I was.

I remembered something Les Brown once said: *"You don't have to be great to start, but you have to get started to be great."*[1] So here I am.

And this… is my story.

Chapter 1:
My Childhood

For most of my childhood, my world was small and fragile. It consisted of my mother, my little sister, and me—three people trying to survive with very little stability and even fewer answers.

My biological father left when I was very young. So young that I have only scattered memories and a couple of faded photographs to prove he was ever part of my life. A Filipino man and a young Black woman fell in love, married, and had me. I emphasize *young* because my father was forty-two and my mother was only twenty-two at the time—a twenty-year age gap, two cultures colliding, two very different life experiences trying to coexist.

My sister was born shortly after, and then everything unraveled.

What truly happened between my parents is something I still don't fully know. Bits and pieces surfaced years later, but the whole truth never came together. As a child, I assumed my father didn't care. Absence feels like rejection when you're young, and silence answers questions no one explains. I grew up hearing only one side of the story, and even that version never quite added up. No matter the circumstances, I believed a father should love his child. Yet he was gone—and with him went a sense of belonging I didn't yet know how to name.

At the time, I called it bad luck.

Being biracial added another layer of confusion. To this day, half of who I am feels like a mystery. I know nothing about my Filipino heritage—no language, no traditions, no foods passed down through generations. That entire side of me feels like a locked room I was never invited into. All I knew was Chicago. The West Side. Poverty. Instability. Dysfunction that masqueraded as normal because it was all I had ever seen.

Let me say this clearly: I am proud to be Black. I come from a people who have endured oppression, survived injustice, and still rise with strength, beauty, and resilience. Black men and women are powerful, intelligent, creative, and fierce. I love who God made me to be. And yet—for much of my life—I didn't understand *who* I was. Something felt missing deep inside, and not knowing your identity creates a quiet ache that follows you everywhere.

Whenever I asked my mother about my father, she brushed it aside. "You're better off without him," she'd say. End of discussion. In Black households, certain questions aren't encouraged. You learn quickly what not to ask.

My sister—three years younger—shared my last name but not my father.

Another unanswered question. Two little girls growing up without fathers. One single mother who often spoke about how unloved she felt as a child herself, now trying to raise us alone while carrying her own unresolved pain.

We moved constantly. Different schools. Different states. Apartments, shelters, relatives' homes. Nothing ever seemed permanent. I remember walking long distances in the cold, not knowing where we were going or how long we'd stay once we arrived. When we did have a place of our own, it never lasted. Eviction notices taped to doors. Our belongings were piled outside. Those images etched themselves into my memory and followed me well into adulthood.

I'm not here to shame anyone. But choices—intentional or not—shape children. I know my mother tried. I truly believe she did the best she could with what she had and knew. But effort without healing still leaves wounds. Stability mattered more to me than space. I would have gladly lived in a tiny studio if it meant knowing where we'd sleep at night. What hurt most was watching people grow tired of taking us in and then sending us back out into the cold.

School was no refuge. My mind was always racing, always worried. Concentration felt impossible. I already felt like an outsider, and bullying made sure I never forgot it. My lighter skin and long hair made me a target in predominantly Black schools. Trouble seemed to stalk me everywhere—before school, during school, and after. Once again, I labeled it bad luck.

My sister and I didn't get along either. She resented me, believing I received more attention from our mother. From my perspective, she was the favorite, embraced by family because she looked like them. I felt like a stranger in my own bloodline. We resented each other for things neither of us had any control over.

My mother gave what she considered to be love, but true love, consistency, and emotional safety were concepts she had never fully learned herself. I grew up watching her argue endlessly with her own mother. Alcohol, anger, and chaos were familiar companions. Weekends meant parties where kids watched too much, heard too much, and learned too much too soon. Grandma's house could be fun, but it wasn't safe.

Alcohol is a powerful spirit, and I watched it turn laughter into rage.

One night still lives vividly in my body.

It was dark. My mother missed curfew at the shelter. She whispered for us to stay low; to cover ourselves so no one would see us. I remember being wrapped tightly in a blanket, lying still in the car, staring up at the stars through the window. I was young. Afraid. Helpless. Yet somehow, those stars made me feel protected. I didn't know it then, but God was already watching over me.

Through everything, my mother stayed with us. She never gave us away. If there was only one bed, she slept on the floor so we could be comfortable. I honor her for that. She tried. But something always held her back—something unhealed, something unresolved. I cried as I wrote this because I saw her struggle. I saw her potential. I saw how cycles repeat when they're never broken.

And then, when I was five years old, God brought someone into my life who brought a glimmer of hope.

He didn't have to stay.

But he did.

And his story comes next.

Chapter 2:
Paul, Also Known as Dad

Change entered my life quietly—not as a dramatic moment, but as a person. His name was Paul.

He wasn't perfect—no one is—but he was willing. Willing to step into a life already tangled with instability. Willing to help my mother raise two small girls who were not his biological children, while carrying his own responsibilities and burdens. Looking back now, with the lens of faith, I see that willingness as an early sign of God's provision—appearing long before I knew how to recognize it.

I remember the first day I met Paul, which still surprises me because I don't remember meeting any of my mother's other boyfriends. That day stands apart. My mother was dressed beautifully, glowing in a way I rarely saw. She was smiling—truly smiling. When we walked in, Paul didn't loom over us. He knelt down to our level. I was five or six; my sister was three or four. His posture was gentle, his voice calm. He greeted us as though we mattered.

Paul recorded that meeting on video. I still have the footage tucked away in my closet. On it, he asks us our ages, what we liked, and what made us laugh. He showed us a large piano, and we eagerly pressed the keys, filling the room with clumsy music. The camera lingered on my mother as she watched us play. She blushed, laughed shyly, and for a moment looked unburdened. Paul adored her. Even through the lens, his love was unmistakable.

For a time, Paul and my mother dated on and off. Eventually, we moved in with him, and life felt steady, until it didn't. Their relationship was volatile. Paul had three children of his own, and while we got to know them, family life was never settled. Arguments were frequent. My mother, shaped by her own painful upbringing, responded to conflict with anger and destruction. Paul was soft-spoken and patient, sometimes to his own detriment.

The relationship was further complicated by unfinished marriages. Paul eventually finalized his divorce. My mother did not. Still, Paul remained—waiting, hoping, loving. At the time, I didn't understand why he stayed. Now I believe love, when mixed with brokenness, often keeps people where wisdom might not.

Through it all, Paul showed up for us.

One Christmas remains etched in my memory. Paul brought home a real tree and decorated it carefully. To my sister and me, it was breathtaking. During an argument, my mother knocked it over and said, without hesitation, "No one is going to have Christmas in here." Ornaments shattered across the floor. We cried. Paul didn't raise his voice. He simply stood there, absorbing the moment. Even then, I saw a quiet strength in him—a restraint that felt foreign in a world where anger usually won.

I witnessed unhealthy patterns between my mother and Paul—patterns I later recognized as generational. While Paul was not without fault, I never saw him strike her. He endured much and forgave often. As an adult, I understand they were two wounded people trying to build something neither had the tools to sustain. Sometimes love alone is not enough.

Still, Paul remained a constant presence. Even after separations, he continued to show up for us. His consistency gave me a glimpse of stability I hadn't known before. I now believe God was using Paul to show me what faithfulness could look like in imperfect form.

When we lived in Rogers Park, life felt almost ordinary. We had a stable apartment, family nearby, and laughter filled our days. Paul often talked to us about school, discipline, purpose, and boys. His favorite phrase was, "Knowledge is power." At the time, I rolled my eyes. Today, I hear those words as a seed planted long before I was ready to receive it.

As instability returned, Paul's presence faded—not by his choice, but because of circumstances beyond his control. That absence left a void. Searching for love in the wrong places, I made decisions that altered the course of my life. At sixteen, I became pregnant. The disappointment on Paul's face was something I'll never forget. It wasn't anger—it was heartbreak.

Yet even then, he didn't turn away.

That is why Paul is my dad.

Looking back now through the lens of faith, I understand that God often sends people into our lives not as permanent fixtures, but as vessels—tools He uses to protect, guide, and love us when we cannot yet see Him clearly.

Paul was one of those vessels. Long before I learned how to trust God, God was already watching over me.

Chapter 3: Kaniya

By late 2007, life was once again shifting beneath my feet. We were not yet living with Dad, but we would be soon. He and my mother were not officially together, yet they were closer than they had been in years. Looking back, I believe Dad simply wanted her near—whether romance was possible or not. He had waited through years of chaos, believing she might one day change. He rarely dated anyone else. His loyalty, though admirable, often cost him peace.

At the same time, my sister and I were growing older, more independent—or so it seemed. My mother had begun allowing us more freedom, partly because she was exhausted, partly because she was distracted by her own relationships, and partly because she believed it was inevitable. We were old enough to dress ourselves, cook small meals, and wander outside. What waited for us out there was not freedom, but influence. Attention. Validation. And for me, boys.

FAITH STRONGER THAN BULLETS | 13

I didn't want rebellion. I wanted to be seen. I wanted to be chosen. I wanted to feel loved.

That longing led me to Chico, a boy I first met when I was just twelve. He was older, confident, charming, and carried himself like someone who belonged to the streets. I mistook that confidence for safety. Over the years, we crossed paths again and again, until finally, at sixteen, our lives reconnected in a way that would forever alter mine.

I did not yet understand how easily trust could be misplaced, or how costly certain decisions could become. I believed affection meant commitment. I believed words meant protection. I was wrong.

Not long afterward, my body began to change in ways I couldn't ignore. When I discovered I was pregnant, the world seemed to stop. I was sixteen years old—still a child myself—and carrying a life I was not prepared for.

Telling my mother was one of the hardest moments of my life. I could barely lift my eyes as tears spilled down my face. She knew before I finished speaking. The weight of disappointment filled the room, and with it, fear—especially fear of telling Dad. I had failed the one man who had spent years warning me, guiding me, and loving me as his own.

Living under his roof again while pregnant was unbearable. His silence was louder than words. When he finally spoke, the disappointment cut deep, but even then, his concern was not cruelty. It was grief. Grief for a future he had hoped would be different for me.

There was discussion of ending the pregnancy. That conversation broke something open inside of me. Alone in a car with my mother one day, I wept. Not from fear, but from clarity. I had already bonded with the life growing inside me. I didn't know much then, but I knew this: I could not let go of my child.

And so, without fully understanding the road ahead, I chose life.

The baby's father faded from my world not long after. His calls slowed, then stopped. I was left to wrestle with abandonment—something I knew all too well. Yet even in that loneliness, God was quietly working, though I didn't recognize His hand at the time.

Later, I met someone else. He was kind, gentle, and unexpectedly willing to stand beside me. He did not judge me or pressure me. His family welcomed me. For the first time in a long while, I felt supported. I did not expect him to raise my child, nor did I want to burden him with a responsibility that was not his. But his presence softened the fear I carried.

As my pregnancy progressed, provision came from unexpected places. Family members helped prepare for the baby. Supplies filled the room—diapers, clothes, a bassinet. My mother, though conflicted, began to love the idea of her first grandchild. Dad, slowly, began to soften. He never stopped teaching, never stopped reminding me that responsibility had arrived.

Then, on September 6, 2008, after a long yet bearable labor, my daughter was born.

When the nurses placed her in my arms, everything changed.

Fear gave way to awe. Shame dissolved into purpose. I stared at this tiny, perfect life and felt a love so powerful it erased the past and silenced the future's worries—if only for a moment. She had soft black hair, gentle eyes, and a presence that filled the room. I named her Kaniya—a name as unique as the miracle she was.

Holding her, I made a promise: I would love her fiercely. I would protect her. I would break the cycle.

Her biological father did not come because I denied access to my room and my baby. I grieved that quietly because I was not alone. My Dad eventually came and held his granddaughter with tenderness. My family gathered around us. And somehow, in the midst of fear and uncertainty, I felt something unfamiliar—hope.

Motherhood had arrived before I was ready. But God, in His mercy, had arrived before I even knew I needed Him.

Three days into being a mother, the rest of my life began.

Chapter 4:
Jeremiah

Life had settled into a rhythm for a while. I had a beautiful, healthy baby girl, Kaniya, and my parents were helping me care for her. My boyfriend and his family also supported me, allowing me to focus on finishing my last year of high school. I got my first job at McDonald's when Kaniya was around five or six months old. It was just part-time, and the pay was minimum wage—seven twenty-five an hour back then—but I felt proud buying diapers, clothes, and necessities for my little girl. Everyone continued to help because they saw how hard I was working—juggling school, a job, and motherhood. My boyfriend watched Kaniya sometimes while I worked, and I was grateful. He was attentive and patient with her, and I appreciated that.

As high school graduation approached, I balanced preparing for prom, finishing classes, and caring for Kaniya, who was nearly nine months old.

Despite everything, I managed to earn A's and B's, placing within the Top Twenty of my class—a group of students recognized for hard work, intelligence, and determination. Even amid its challenges, the Westside of Chicago was full of young people striving for success. I was proud of myself. I had a child, I was managing school, and I hadn't given up.

I received a small scholarship to Roosevelt University's downtown campus, but living on campus with Kaniya wasn't feasible, so I planned to start at a community college. But life had other plans. Within weeks, I discovered I was pregnant again. Kaniya wasn't even one year old. I was about to bring another life into the world while still learning what it meant to be a mother.

Adding to the challenge, my little sister—three years younger than me—was also expecting a child at fifteen. She was slightly ahead of me in pregnancy, and I felt guilty as a big sister. We hadn't been close, and I worried I wasn't setting a good example. My sister had felt overlooked when I had Kaniya, and now she was navigating her own journey.

During this time, we were all living with Dad. One could only imagine the weight of his disappointment. He had tried so hard to guide us, yet we hadn't followed his advice. Mom had mostly stepped back, giving us space, and my sister moved in with a relative and then I too moved, but with my boyfriend and his family. Dad and Mom still loved us, but it was clear their patience had limits. With maturity, I can now fully understand their perspective.

I was grateful for my boyfriend and his family, who welcomed Kaniya and me into their home. They provided stability, support, and love, but I soon realized how unprepared I was for the responsibilities I had taken on. My boyfriend was working, attending school, and helping care for two children while I relied on public assistance to help meet our basic needs.

The weight of it all was heavy.

My second child, a son named Jeremiah, arrived on February 26, 2010—just a day before the baby shower we had planned. I went into labor early that morning, and my boyfriend helped me get to the hospital. Kaniya stayed behind with his mother until my mother could watch her and my Dad would soon come when he was available. I tried for a natural birth again, but eventually asked for an epidural. After hours of labor, Jeremiah was born healthy, weighing seven pounds. Holding him in my arms for the first time was overwhelming. I couldn't believe I now had a son, and the love I felt for him instantly shifted my perspective. My children were my priority, and I resolved to give them the care and devotion I wished I had received as a child.

Though Jeremiah's father was present during the birth and attentive in the beginning, the challenges of young parenthood quickly became apparent.

Balancing work, school, and two young children was overwhelming. Slowly, his presence in our daily lives faded. It wasn't bitterness that drove me, but the reality that he simply wasn't ready for the responsibility. In time, I moved forward, supported by family, while hurt, but needing to get away not fully knowing what to expect.

With my parents' help, I found a place of my own, secured a job, and attended Harold Washington College. I started building a life independently, striving to be the mother and role model my children needed. My sister also had a healthy baby, and I helped care for him so she could finish school. Despite initial challenges, we learned to support each other and embrace our responsibilities. Both of us were young mothers, still growing, still learning—but determined to give our children a better foundation than we had experienced.

Looking back, I see God's hand in every step of this journey. The trials, the mistakes, the heartache—they were all part of the story He was writing in my life. My children became my motivation to rise above circumstances, to seek guidance from Him, and to trust in His plan for our family. Through it all, I learned that faith, perseverance, and love could break cycles and build hope for the next generation.

Chapter 5: Chico

It was 2011. Kaniya was three, and Jeremiah was one. Living on my own with two small children while attending college and working was challenging. I was getting by, but barely. Keeping a roof over our heads was everything. We lived in a modest one-bedroom apartment in the city; the rent was $600, and while the building had its flaws, it was livable—at least for a time. Having a washer and dryer in the building made life easier, but eventually the conditions worsened, and I had to move. I didn't care where, as long as my children had a safe home.

One day, while sitting alone and thinking about Kaniya's future since my now ex-boyfriend only wanted to raise his child and his child only after everything we created together, I realized she needed to know at least who her father was. Her biological father had been arrested in 2008, and I had no communication with him since. I knew she deserved to know him.

With a mix of hope and apprehension, I decided to introduce them.

When Chico saw Kaniya for the first time, he was shocked. She looked just like him. And though he was behind bars, she somehow instinctively knew he was her daddy. That moment—the warmth in her smile, the spark of recognition—made the harshness of the surroundings fade away. The visiting area was stark, filled with other families, glass partitions, and the hum of regulated chaos. Yet, for that brief moment, nothing else mattered.

Visiting Chico became a ritual. What began as a quest for answers turned into a connection born of longing and shared vulnerability. I had always had a soft spot for him, and in the loneliness of my life, I found comfort in these visits. "Jail love," some called it—love nurtured in absence, hope sustained by letters and fleeting conversations. I gave him hope, he gave me reassurance, and together we imagined a future once he was released.

Chico's sentence was fair—eleven years at fifty percent, meaning he would only have to serve six and a half years total. He served most of that in the county jail and freedom was near. In May 2014, that future became real.

Driving to the facility that morning, I felt a mix of excitement and nerves. Kaniya, bright and eager, sensed what was about to happen. When the doors opened, she ran into her father's arms, and for the first time, their connection wasn't behind glass or regulated by rules. She clung to him as if she had known him all her life. The joy in that moment was overwhelming. Even Jeremiah took a moment to warm up, but soon laughter filled the car as Chico marveled at the children—children he had not raised but now had the chance to know.

Returning home, reality set in. Chico couldn't legally stay at my apartment yet, so he initially lived with his aunt and commuted to see us. The first days were quiet, the house nearly empty, and I worried: did he know how to be a father outside of visiting hours? But he was patient, willing to learn, and devoted to his children. He attended all required classes, complied with his parole requirements, and embraced the small victories.

As the months passed, Chico faced the challenge of freedom. After six years behind bars, the world outside was foreign. There were temptations, distractions, and a sense of unrestrained choice. For a while, he tested boundaries, seeking independence in ways I couldn't anticipate. But I had reached my limit. When I confronted him, I spoke clearly and with conviction: "Chico, I love you, but I can't do this alone anymore. The kids and I deserve stability, and one day, we will receive it from someone who chooses to stay."

That moment became a turning point. Chico took responsibility. He moved fully into our home, sought work, and became the father my children needed. Slowly, the house that had been quiet and uncertain transformed into a home filled with laughter, learning, and hope. He found employment at Cooper's Hawk Winery in Oak Lawn, starting humbly as a dishwasher but proving his worth through hard work and dedication. Within months, he earned promotions, bringing a sense of pride and security to our family.

Soon after, we learned we were expecting another child. Despite the challenges of finances and responsibilities, our hearts were full. Life wasn't perfect, but we were together, learning how to love, forgive, and navigate adulthood as partners and parents. Arguments came and went, as they do in any family, but our commitment to our children and each other strengthened us. Chico never harmed our children. His patience and tenderness with them became the foundation of trust and love in our home.

Even when family misunderstandings arose—rumors about our household or doubts cast by relatives—Chico maintained grace. He did not allow bitterness to take root. Eventually, my sister, who had been skeptical at first, saw the love and care we had for our children and apologized for her assumptions. Relationships healed, and our household found peace.

We had endured struggles, learned lessons, and grown together. Our children were thriving, and for the first time, I felt confident in the life we were building. We were young, imperfect, and learning as we went, but through perseverance and commitment, we were creating a family rooted in love.

Chapter 6: Eman

Our relationship wasn't perfect, but it had its moments—the kind you replay in your head forever. Like my twenty-fourth birthday. Chico spent his last couple of dollars on a cruise at Navy Pier. It was July in Chicago. The warm breeze, the lights of the city reflecting on the calm waters, the stars above—it felt like the world had paused just for us. I lay in Chico's arms as he whispered, "I love you," and for that moment, nothing else existed.

Earlier that day, he had gotten my hair done, bought our outfits, and secured two tickets for the cruise. He had a knack for little gestures that made life sweeter. When I had long days at work, he would have dinner ready, the house tidy, and a bath drawn for me. The kids would be asleep or playing with him on the Xbox, and all was peaceful. He even involved his older son, and I loved seeing them all together, smiling and laughing.

Then came this pregnancy. Like the others, it was unplanned, but this time, fear crept in. Early in my pregnancy, two doctors told me I was likely to miscarry. Blood had been detected around the fetus, and they warned of the worst. Complete bed rest was the only option if there was any hope. But I refused to accept it. My baby was mine, and I knew he would live. Bed rest wasn't an option—we had bills to pay, kids to care for, lives to manage. I trusted my instincts.

Months passed. Each doctor's appointment confirmed my hope: the baby was thriving. On May 29, 2015, my water broke around seven in the morning. Contractions followed immediately, relentless and intense. Chico sprang into action, getting Kaniya and Jeremiah ready and driving us to the hospital. I felt as though my body was being torn apart, piece by piece, but I refused to panic. He called his aunt and grandmother to get the kids while I went upstairs.

By the time they checked me, I was already seven centimeters dilated. I begged for an epidural. The anesthesiologist was delayed, and the pain was excruciating, but finally, relief came. Chico was racing up in the elevator, a mix of worry and excitement on his face. And then, in six pushes, Eman entered the world—a beautiful, calm, over-seven-pound baby boy. Chico, unfortunately, missed the birthing process and ran in just in time as the doctor laid our baby on my chest, but his joy was palpable when he saw him. Nurses cleaned Eman, ran tests, and allowed Kaniya and Jeremiah to meet their new brother under careful supervision. That first day, the house of our hearts expanded again.

Two days later, we were home. Life reset with two small children, a newborn's needs, and the endless rhythm of motherhood. I found a new job at Home Depot, perfectly scheduled around Chico's night shifts. We were managing, growing, surviving—but life had its next challenge waiting.

Chico wanted extra money. Despite a steady job, he started selling small amounts of weed. I voiced my objections, but he reassured me, insisting it was harmless. Foolishly, I believed him.

We lived in Auburn Gresham on the South Side—a seemingly quiet area. But the world outside our doors was far from safe. Gunshots, robberies, and violence unfolded nightly, often in plain view. One evening, I watched a man sprint to a car after gunfire. The news was dominated by shootings. Yet we carried on, believing that as long as we kept to ourselves, we would be fine. Chico worked hard, exercised daily, supported the family, and handled the small side hustle. Life was messy, chaotic, and dangerous—but we were surviving, together.

Chapter 7:
A Warning from God

It was early February 2016. Kaniya, Jeremiah, and Eman were growing fast, their personalities blossoming every day. Chico and I were still together. We still bumped heads—sometimes loudly, sometimes silently—but our arguments no longer shook the foundation of our home. We could debate until the sun came up and then laugh about it a minute later.

Across the hall in our two-story building lived someone we both adored: Lady B. She was a neighbor, but she was so much more—mentor, friend, counselor, and mother figure all rolled into one. Whenever I needed space, a break from Chico, or simply someone to listen, I would find my way to her apartment. Lady B had a way of cutting through the chaos of our young lives. She could see through our stubbornness and tell us the hard truths with honesty and love. She would sit us down, remind us to co-parent, to grow, to get our act together, and somehow, even when we thought we were done, we would leave feeling better, lighter, and a little wiser. She never left us, no matter what else was happening. And whenever she needed us, we were always there.

Then came the neighbor who would later weave into our story in a way I couldn't yet understand. Chico began spending time with a Filipino man who moved in nearby, along with his wild nephew. At first, he seemed like a decent person, but within weeks, they had moved out—the nephew caught up in neighborhood gang drama. I include this because it matters later.

One ordinary January or February day, after work, I walked up to our front door. The air was cold, the streets quiet, no snow—just another regular day. But then it happened. I froze. And for the first time in my life, I had a vision.

I saw three bullets fly toward me from behind—slow motion, crystal clear, aimed near my lower back. It was cinematic, like something from a movie, but horrifyingly real. My body trembled, my mind screamed disbelief. I unfroze, fumbling with the keys, climbed the steps to our apartment, and stumbled inside, dazed. Chico was there, sitting, looking confused, while I paced like a ghost. I'm not sure if I told him at that moment—my memory is blurred—but the vision shook me to my core.

For days, I couldn't shake it. Yet life moved forward, as it always does. I picked up Eman, who smiled innocently from his bouncer, and I tried to believe it was over.

Weeks went by. February 24th and 25th brought arguments, the kind that start small and escalate. Lady B intervened, insisting I leave with the kids for a drive while she calmed Chico down. As we rode, I imagined leaving him for good—moving to Wisconsin with my sister. It was a fleeting thought, but it felt like breathing. I was embarrassed even to consider it.

What were we fighting about? I couldn't tell you if my life depended on it.

Lady B drove slowly, gently, while I absorbed her words. She didn't scold, didn't judge. She reminded me that our children saw everything and absorbed more than we realized. "Do better," she said, simply. At that moment, I understood: Chico and I were missing the number one thing we both needed—God.

That night, back home, Lady B asked if we wanted to stay over. I declined, wanting to return to my own space. Chico apologized, I nodded silently, and I laid the children down. I curled up with them, exhausted, physically and emotionally drained. Arguments over. For now.

February 26th arrived—Jeremiah's sixth birthday. I slept in the children's room, and Chico apologized again the next morning. I didn't respond. Words failed me. He suggested we set aside the tension and focus on preparing for Jeremiah's party at the Martin Luther King Center on Racine Street. The kids' excitement was the only thing that mattered. We had nothing ready: no outfits, no favors, no cake. Yet somehow, we rallied.

We shopped, prepped, and hustled. By party time, the kids glowed, and so did we, in spite of the lingering tension. Pizza, wings, candy, laughter, skating, and bowling—Jeremiah's joy made the chaos worthwhile. His father and family were there too, and despite initial awkwardness, we all focused on him, on family, on love.

The evening ended, and Jeremiah asked to spend the weekend with his father. I let him go, weary, eager for my bed and the comfort of quiet. I begged Chico to skip the gym for once, just to stay with us. He promised only an hour—but whether he left or stayed, I barely registered. And in hindsight, that night would mark our last day together as we knew it.

Chapter 8: Ambushed with Bullets

The morning of February 27th arrived like any other Saturday, yet something felt… different. Heavenly. Peaceful. Light poured into our apartment, so bright it nearly blinded us as we threw open the blinds. I didn't know why, but the warmth filled me with a rare sense of calm, as if the world had paused just for a moment. How ironic, I would soon realize.

I awoke feeling refreshed, renewed, as though I'd never felt this alive before. The apartment was quiet, still, almost sacred in its calm. I crept through the rooms to check on the kids. They slept peacefully, and Jeremiah's bed was empty—it felt strange, almost disorienting. I returned to our bedroom and watched Chico. He lay there; the only moment he seemed truly at peace. Six years locked away had left scars, and life's unending demands had shaped him into someone who carried the weight of everyone around him. Money, advice, a shoulder to cry on—he always showed up.

Chico stirred awake and immediately wrapped me in his arms. "I love you," he whispered. I replied in kind. He began apologizing for the tension of the past few days, confessing he hadn't been himself. I simply said, "It's okay," wanting only to heal him with love.

Kaniya appeared then, cradling seven-month-old Eman, gently placing him in the bed. She climbed under the covers beside me, snuggling close. Chico joined in, tickling and kissing Eman until he laughed, and then passed him to me. He tickled Kaniya's belly and whispered, "I love you." In that moment, all I wanted was a family—my children to grow up knowing their father in a safe, loving home. We weren't perfect. We didn't always know God. We had our flaws. But we were trying.

The day began in ordinary fashion. I took the kitchen duties while Chico tidied the house. The smell of rice, eggs, bacon, and fresh fruit mingled with the warm sunlight streaming through the blinds. Eman walked happily in his walker as Kaniya chased him around, their laughter echoing through our home. I was off work, and Chico would be home until the evening, so we enjoyed the rare luxury of time together as a family.

Around ten a.m., a knock at the door startled us. It was Lady B.

"Dang!" she exclaimed as she stepped inside.

"What's wrong?" I asked, smiling.

"It's brighter than I've ever seen it in here! And look at you with that vacuum, young man!"

We laughed, and I helped her carry trays of food to her car. She complimented us on our energy and left for her event. The winter weather was cold but tolerable—still, the light that filled the apartment stayed with me.

By early afternoon, we were dressed and ready to run errands. Chico first stopped at his "Weed Man." I watched with quiet disapproval but said nothing. I stayed in the car with the kids as he hopped into another vehicle. Once that errand was done, we stopped at a shrimp place near Simeon High School. I got out to order our food while the kids played, laughter ringing through the air. Finally, we stopped at the store for some personal items, then headed home, the children peaceful and smiling in the backseat.

As we turned onto the 900 block of West 85th Street, everything changed. A man was slowly crossing the street ahead of us. Chico slowed to avoid him, confused. Then, without warning, a boy appeared from an alley near our building—right where I had my vision sometime before.

He raised his arm and began shooting.

Everything moved in slow motion in my mind, yet real bullets tore through our car in a devastating rhythm:

POW! POW! POW!

The bullets kept coming. Glass shattered. Screams erupted. My heart felt like it stopped. I lunged toward the back seat, toward my children, but the Chevy's front seat was a single unit. I dangled, scrambled, and landed back in the passenger seat, a sharp pain exploding in my lower body.

The shooter lowered his weapon and disappeared before my eyes. But the danger wasn't over. The car lurched in reverse.

BOOM!

We crashed into a parked vehicle directly behind us.

My world narrowed to my children. Their screams were piercing, unimaginable. Tears and fear etched across their tiny faces—this was the terror a parent never wants to witness.

And then I turned around and stared at Chico.

He was slumped forward, head down, blood pooling around his nose and mouth. His eyes were closed. The gurgling stopped. My heart stopped with him.

Across the street, neighbors rushed toward us. An older woman and a young lady pulled Kaniya and Eman from the car. Through the blur of fear, I heard Kaniya scream, "Daddy!"

I could not move. Could not speak. I was frozen. Blood coated my hands, my clothes, my purse. A sharp, pulsating pain tore through me. Around us, the neighborhood erupted in chaos—people screaming, crying, rushing to help. One courageous man tried to lift Chico to resuscitate him, pleading,

"Come on! You got this! Get up!"

Paramedics, police, and firefighters arrived almost immediately. A bullet to the head had rendered Chico dead on arrival, right before my eyes. I was lifted from the car, clutching my purse and Chico's phone, texting everyone I could to alert them to the nightmare that had just unfolded. The sirens and chaos blurred around me, but I stayed awake, alert, desperate to make sure my babies were safe.

At the hospital, the world became sterile and cold. Nurses, doctors, and intern students swarmed around me, questioning, testing, and preparing. I answered absent-mindedly, texting frantically. I was alone, terrified, and utterly numb. The pain throbbed, the blood soaked through everything, yet the worst part—the part that would haunt me forever—was the terror in my children's eyes and Chico lying lifeless in that front seat.

Laid flat on a cold, white surgical table, the smell of antiseptic filling my nose, I stared at the ceiling. Tears streamed, and a white mist enveloped me from the mask pressed over my face. My eyelids grew heavy. I felt the exhaustion of trauma and terror, the grief of a world that had just shattered, and I slipped into a sleep I had never known—one I would later realize was a grace, a momentary reprieve from a reality too cruel to bear.

Chapter 9:
Waking Up to My New Life

Beep... beep... beep... beep.

My eyes slowly opened. I was in a hospital, but it took a moment to realize it. I thought it was still the same night, maybe eleven p.m., almost midnight—but years later, one of my surgeons told me twenty-four hours had passed since surgery. All I knew was that I couldn't move. I couldn't speak. My body felt like it no longer belonged to me.

Monitors beeped steadily, a cold, mechanical rhythm that contrasted the chaos I had just survived. My first thought: *my children, my boyfriend—are they okay?* My back and legs refused to move. Tears streamed down my face as the memory hit me—bullets, shattered glass, my life changed in a flash. *Why?*

I was stripped of my clothes and undergarments, left only in a frail hospital gown. My neck and head felt heavy, rigid. Something foreign lay in my throat. I couldn't move freely, couldn't turn my head. Panic set in. I reached up with my right hand; my left was wrapped in heavy white bandages.

I started to explore my body. My head was swaddled in cloth bandages, covering every stitch from under my bottom lip to my chin, almost reaching my right ear. My fingers brushed my mouth—I could feel the metal clamp locking my teeth and gums together. My tongue couldn't move. My lips were swollen, the pain almost unbearable. My hand slid down my throat. Sharp, searing pain hit me: a tracheostomy. A surgically created hole in my windpipe to breathe. Blood had filled my mouth, and I hadn't even realized it.

Moving down my left arm, I lifted it to my eyes. The white bandage covered my hand entirely. I couldn't move my thumb. A bullet had lodged there, fragments embedded in my soft tissue. I pressed on my lower body—the pain I had felt in my private area before was still there, dull but present. A lump the size of a baseball pressed against me, swollen, bruised. I was trapped in my own body, forced to lie helplessly as the monitors beeped their relentless rhythm.

Then, the medical team arrived. Nurses, surgeons, and doctors appeared through the curtains, explaining my injuries. I had already felt them, but hearing the words made it real:

- A bullet had entered and exited my chin, shattering bone and tearing my lower face apart.
- The tracheostomy had been inserted to keep me alive.
- Another bullet had crossed my private area coming in from the right buttock, hitting the lower portion, and exiting through my left leg damaging surrounding tissue.
- My left hand contained bullet fragments. The surgeons explained it was safer to leave them than risk further injury.

I felt numb. My life—my body—had been violated in every way possible. And still, I had questions, urgent ones. *Where were my children? Where was Chico?*

A detective team arrived—four to six officers, their faces etched with shock and empathy. They introduced themselves and began questioning me gently. I answered everything through writing. I told them what I remembered, every detail, every face, every moment. I described the shooter—the anger in his eyes, the hatred radiating from him, the violence that had filled the air. I had caught his face. I would never forget it.

And then I asked, trembling:

"Is Eric… Chico… dead?"

"Yes," they said.

The words tore through me. My face and neck throbbed from crying, but I couldn't stop. My soul felt like it had been ripped out. Everything was surreal—detectives questioning me, nurses bustling around, monitors beeping—but all I could think about was Chico and my children. My world had collapsed in one moment, and now I had to piece it together while trapped in this broken body.

I lay there, numb, broken, barely breathing through the tracheostomy, listening to the constant, mechanical beep of the monitors. Doctors and nurses moved around me like ghosts. I stared at the ceiling, clinging to consciousness as exhaustion, pain, and grief began to pull me under. I was awake, aware, but trapped—frozen in a body that had survived hell.

Finally, the detectives left. I was alone with my pain, my trauma, my grief. I cried myself into a restless sleep, clutching the fragments of my shattered life. My body was wounded. My family was broken. And I had just woken up to a new reality I couldn't yet understand.

Chapter 10: Two Weeks Felt Like Two Decades

Beep... beep... beep... beep.

My eyes fluttered open, and the relentless beeping of the monitors greeted me. I prayed silently, whispering, *Lord, please let this be a bad dream. Let me wake up at home with my children.* But reality hit hard—the sterile hospital walls, the pale glow of fluorescent lights, the pain coursing through my body. I was alive... but barely.

Then I heard a familiar voice. My cousin, her presence a balm to my shattered soul. She worked at Christ Hospital and had come early, using her ID to be with me the moment I woke. I broke down in tears the second I saw her. She hugged me gently and handed me my pen and pad.

The first words I scrawled were desperate, trembling: "Are my kids okay?"

She smiled through her own tears. "Yes, they're with your mother and sister. Jeremiah is still with his father for now. He knows nothing."

My chest tightened, and I hesitated to ask the next question. Slowly, I wrote: "IS CHICO DEAD?"

Her face crumbled. "Yes."

My world exploded. My heart raced, my chest burned, and the monitors blared in warning. I sobbed so violently I could feel my heart in my stomach. God, how could this be? *How could the one I loved, the man who had built a life with me, be gone?*

My cousin held my hand. "Breathe. Please just breathe."

I nodded weakly, tears streaming, and gave thanks for her presence. She became my guardian angel that day, helping me navigate a body that no longer obeyed me, a life that felt like a nightmare.

I was desperate, helpless, and in pain. I had to urinate, and the thought terrified me. How could I manage this without moving? My cousin smiled softly and placed a bedpan beneath me. Every movement, every shift, was agony. Lifting my fragile body, allowing her to assist, I felt humiliated—but also grateful.

And then it repeated. Ten minutes later, again. And again. The nurses soon explained I needed a catheter. I had never felt so vulnerable in my life, but God's grace held me steady. Every step, every procedure, reminded me that even in brokenness, He was with me.

When my family began to arrive, the weight of reality hit me again. Only four people at a time were allowed, but each entrance was heartbreaking. My sister fell to the floor at the sight of me. My father entered, bawling and cursing under his breath, his grief and rage spilling over. My mother's tears fell, and though our history had been stormy, I felt a strange tenderness for her in that moment. They were all shaken, overwhelmed, seeing me so wounded, so small—but alive.

And I thought of my children. My heart ached. My children, my joy, my reason for fighting… I longed to hold them, to tell them *everything would be okay*, though even I did not know if it would be. Every tear I shed, every cry for my babies, felt like fuel for survival. God was using that love to keep me breathing.

Next came the feeding tube. Another invasion, another reminder that I could do nothing for myself. I watched the yellow tube slide into my nose, down my throat, into my stomach. I gagged and cried silently, but I survived each second. Liquid feeding, they said. Hydration and nourishment. God's mercy flows in a strange, mechanical way.

Hours blurred into a rhythm of pain and care: IVs for hydration, blood thinners, antibiotics, pain medicine. Every two hours, someone came to tend to my body, to clean and protect the wounds that had almost claimed my life. The pain in my private area, the trauma from the bullets, was almost unbearable. I screamed through the metal wires that held my jaw shut, wincing with every touch, every cleaning, every movement.

And yet, worse than all the pain was the ache in my soul—the absence of my children, the silence where Chico once was. That emptiness gnawed at me, stronger than the needles, stronger than the tubes, stronger than the blood loss.

Lady B came to visit, her comforting words and prayers wrapping around me. My uncle, a man of deep faith, prayed fervently over me, speaking life into my broken body. Friends, old and new, came tirelessly—Jasmin traveling long hours while pregnant, family members crying, holding my hand, reminding me that love could endure even this.

Yet, there were moments I shut everyone out. I needed solitude to rebuild my strength, to wrestle with grief. Every day was a test of endurance, every hour a step closer to healing.

Time was approaching two weeks—or perhaps two decades. Time no longer mattered. Looking back, every nurse, every doctor, every procedure was a reminder that God had not abandoned me. He was carrying me through, shaping me through fire.

Through the agony, the humiliation, the heartbreak, and the endless tubes, I learned something profound: survival was not just physical—it was spiritual. My heart beat because He willed it. My children would live because He loved them. And I—broken, bleeding, crying—would live to tell this story, to testify of God's mercy, grace, and unwavering presence.

Chapter 11:
Never Got to Say Goodbye & Learning to Walk Again

About a week into my hospital stay, Chico's funeral took place—March 5, 2016. I barely remember that day. There I was, shot, broken, confined to monitors, and utterly helpless. I couldn't leave my bed, couldn't mourn with those around me, couldn't even touch him. The man I loved, the father of my children, my partner in life, was gone—and I had watched it happen.

When officials finally pulled me out of the car that day, all I could do was look at him. My chin, shattered, prevented me from calling his name, from attempting anything. All I could do was leave his side to save my own life.

Later, I learned he had been left in that car for hours while investigations took place. Darkness fell before anyone moved him. And though I want to be thankful for the people who tried to help, I was devastated and confused. I kept thinking: if this had been someone of "importance," CPR, emergency surgery, ambulance lights flashing—someone would have fought for him. But Chico? He was just another Black man shot.

I stayed with him until he could breathe no more, until he was gone. I took bullets with him, felt the shock of the moment, and witnessed the cowardice of a shooter who hid in the shadows, striking without confrontation. That bullet to the left side of his head—most likely fired as he turned to parallel park—ended his life too quickly. It could have been me next. But I survived. Respectfully, I know now I was chosen.

I could not die. It was not my time.

Even now, I feel I never truly got to say goodbye. Chico was cremated, and the children and I were not included in receiving the ashes. Everyone grieves differently, and I cannot fault them, but the loss remains unbearable. I did not allow our children to attend the funeral; Kaniya had just reconnected with her father, and Eman was only seven months old. They had already been through more than enough. But the emptiness his absence left in their lives was immediate. Babies sense what is missing, and Eman would cling to stuffed animals for comfort, a small reminder of what they had lost.

As I lay in my hospital bed, the enormity of my life shifted. I was now a single mother all over again. Life, which had always been difficult, seemed to collapse around me. Two kids without a father. My other child with limited access to his father. And me—fighting for survival, still reeling from loss.

Learning to Walk Again:

After weeks of surgeries, procedures, and heartbreak, it was time to face another battle: learning to walk again. My body, already petite, had lost significant weight—ten to fifteen pounds, maybe more. My legs were numb, my thighs and butt weak. My body had been immobile for days, fed only through tubes, unable to wash, unable to eat normally. I felt filthy, embarrassed, and utterly dependent. My hair matted with dried blood, my skin unwashed, my breath foul, my private area traumatized.

On the ninth day, a physical therapist arrived—a kind, patient woman who would guide me back to mobility. I apologized for my appearance and odor, but she cared only for helping me stand. With her support, I sat up, scooted my legs over the edge of the bed, and prepared to rise. My body trembled. My muscles refused commands. The simple act of standing felt monumental.

With a walker, deep breaths, and a heart focused on my children, I managed to lift myself. One foot forward. Then the next. I sat back down, exhausted but exhilarated. Each attempt brought me closer to reclaiming the life my body had forgotten.

The next day, she returned. My heart raced with anticipation and fear. Each step was a triumph and a terror. The hallway stretched endlessly. I clutched rails, gripping my fear as tightly as my walker. At one point, the world faded to a white light, and I felt weightless, hovering on the edge between consciousness and release. For a moment, I thought I was entering heaven—peaceful, calm, welcoming. But God was not finished with me. I blinked, and I was back in a chair, dizzy but alive, heart pounding. My children were still waiting for me.

Rediscovering Cleanliness:

Later, a simple shower became another battle for freedom and dignity. Assisted into a walk-in shower with a chair, I painstakingly removed my padding and gently cleaned my wounds. Blood, dried from the car accident, flowed down the drain, along with tears I hadn't realized were still falling. I washed from head to toe, carefully navigating the metal wires holding my jaw, the fragile wounds in my private areas, and the tubes still in place. Every knot, every scrub brought pain—but also a sense of renewal. For the first time, I felt my soul begin to wash away the tragedy, even as my heart remained heavy with grief.

Exhausted, I returned to bed, applying hospital lotion, feeling clean, refreshed, and renewed in a way that only small victories in survival can bring. Sleep came, unforced, and for the first time in days, I allowed myself to rest, the memories of bullets, of Chico, of my children, and of survival lingering like shadows.

Every day in that hospital was a battle. Every step, every breath, every tear was a testament to life, resilience, and the unrelenting desire to hold on—for my children, for my family, for myself.

Chapter 12: Leaving Christ Hospital

Advocate Christ Medical Center was both a blessing and a place of profound darkness for me during nearly two weeks of recovery. Hospitals, by nature, are intimidating and often associated with pain and loss—and my experience was no exception. I endured unimaginable trauma, two near-death experiences, and the aftermath of being shot multiple times. Yet, through it all, I was surrounded by an extraordinary team of caregivers who fought alongside me to preserve my life.

When I arrived at the hospital, battered and bleeding, one of the first people I encountered was Trisha—a remarkable Surgical Coordinator, Anesthesia Assistant, and Dental Hygienist. I didn't know her then, but she remembers arriving with her team in the emergency room to assist Dr. Sinha. Dr. Sinha became my angel on Earth, the surgeon who would painstakingly reconstruct my face. With meticulous precision, he and his team placed stitches, wires, screws, and a metal plate—each element essential to my survival. Without that plate, my jaw would have collapsed; without the wires, my teeth and gums would have been lost. Without the tracheostomy, I could have drowned in my own blood. Their work was nothing short of a miracle.

I don't recall every doctor who treated every wound, especially my private areas or other fractures—but I am profoundly grateful. The staff cared deeply, and their expertise was evident in every procedure. Trisha, in particular, checked on me consistently, updating me with photos of my post-surgical progress and offering reassurance. Days later, I met Dr. Sinha in person. Both of them, alongside their team, saved my life, and I remain in contact with them to this day, sending letters and gratitude that I had not expressed in the years following my trauma. I am committed to honoring their dedication for the rest of my life.

By the end of my stay, I was walking around my room independently, driven by the thought of seeing my children, who I had been told were anxiously waiting for me every day. Each tear I had shed, every pang of anger, every ounce of pain only strengthened my determination to recover.

The day of my discharge, I was overwhelmed with emotion. Minutes dragged by like hours as I prepared myself for the moment I would finally leave, for the moment I would face my children and break the news of Chico's death.

Kaniya already knew that her father had passed, though at seven years old, she could not fully comprehend death. Jeremiah, unaware of the tragedy, believed his parents were simply at the doctor's office for a "tummy ache." Video chats, without showing my face or speaking, but waving, with my sister kept me connected to them during those weeks.

Unfortunately, nothing compared to holding them in my arms.

It was around nine o'clock that evening when I was finally ready to leave. My belongings had been packed hours earlier, and I had fresh clothes provided by my friend Jasmin—joggers and a shirt, which barely fit my weakened frame. I washed up as best I could, combed my tangled hair, and sat in anticipation, as if preparing for a long-awaited reunion. Every movement, every preparation, reminded me of how far I had come and how much further I had to go.

With the assistance of a nurse, I was placed in a wheelchair, my belongings secured behind me. My suction machine, essential for managing saliva from my wired jaw, could not be used in the vehicle, so a stack of paper towels accompanied me to manage the inevitable mess. My cousin met me outside and, with the help of a kind gentleman, lifted me into her car. We drove to my mother's small studio near 76th and Halsted—back to the neighborhood where I had been shot, a place filled with memories, both painful and precious. This was temporary housing, a short-term solution while I awaited subsidized housing in another state. I had no other choice; I could not burden anyone else with our care.

As we approached the apartment, my mother came downstairs and immediately burst into tears. I could not climb the fifteen to twenty steps on my own, so she and my cousin carried me inside. My cousin had to leave shortly afterward, and I held her tightly, overwhelmed with gratitude for her support. Once inside, I was reunited with my children. Kaniya and Jeremiah ran toward the chair I had been placed in, screaming, while Eman's face lit up with pure joy. I held them close, feeling both the weight of my pain and the overwhelming relief of being home.

We settled on the bed, and the full reality of our loss became unavoidable. Jeremiah, confused and anxious, asked, "Where is Chico? When is he coming home? Does his stomach hurt? What is that stuff on you?" Kaniya, on the verge of speaking, was stopped by me as I gently placed my finger over her lips. Through my wired jaw and with tears streaming down my face, I said as clearly as possible, "Baby... Ch... Chico... not coming back. He's g... gone. He... went to heaven w... with God." Jeremiah's breath caught, and he fell to the floor, clutching his chest and sobbing. Kaniya followed in tears. I quickly gathered them in my arms, cradling them as best I could, reassuring them while silently fighting my own heartbreak. Eman, too young to understand, simply smiled in my mother's arms, offering a glimmer of joy amidst the devastation. That moment—their presence, their innocence, their need for comfort—reminded me why I had survived.

During my hospital stay, I had been approved for subsidized housing in another state, offering a fresh start. It was a lifeline, providing hope for the future even as we navigated grief and recovery. For the interim, the small studio on the Southside of Chicago became our home. The space was modest, and the woman I stayed with was not someone I liked- due to the previous chaos and lies she was spreading, but it was temporary. What mattered most was that we were together, alive, and moving forward.

Note to Christ Hospital and Staff:

To the entire staff at Advocate Christ Medical Center who cared for me during those harrowing weeks: from the bottom of my heart, thank you. To those whose care, compassion, and professionalism made my recovery possible—thank you for your time, your skill, and your dedication. If you remember me, or if you are reading this now, know this: you were angels sent from Heaven. Because of you, I was able to return to my beautiful children, stronger, alive, and determined. Thank you, from the deepest part of my soul.

Chapter 13:
A Visit from the Other Side

The first night home was both a blessing and a trial. The kids, exhausted from the joy of having me back, were finally asleep. I settled into the large black couch chair my mother had, the same way I had slept in the hospital—upright, propped with pillows around my neck, back, and sides. Lying down was impossible with the metal in my mouth and the tube in my throat. My suction machine hummed quietly beside me, still a lifeline I depended on.

The feeding tube had been removed before discharge, and it felt like a miracle. I was now on a liquid diet, navigating a tiny hole through my wires that allowed liquid to flow slowly through a straw. For the weeks to come, my world consisted of milkshakes, fruit and vegetable smoothies, and broth-like soups. Every sip was both sustenance and a reminder of my body's fragility.

One night—though I cannot recall if it was the first, second, or third—a presence visited me. A visit I can only describe as spiritual: Chico himself. During my hospital stay, I had begged, silently, for him to come—to give answers, to explain the incomprehensible. But nothing came. Now, at my mother's house, it happened.

I was sitting upright on the couch, caught between sleep and consciousness, when I felt it: an encounter that defied reason. It began like a dream, yet it was more than that—a spiritual experience, a crossing of boundaries I did not understand.

We were on the phone, Chico and I, but the space around us was an endless, black void. Separate, yet together.

In tears, I asked, "Chico, why do you keep leaving me? Why do you keep leaving us? Please… tell me why."

Though we could not see each other on the phone, I could see him clearly, as if his face were illuminated before me. My spirit hovered, watching the scene unfold from above, detached from my physical body yet fully present. His face was a mask of grief. He held the phone close, silent tears running down his cheeks.

"I… don't know, Kashe. I don't know. I just don't know."

My spirit recoiled back into my body as I gasped for air, tears streaming freely. My heart raced; my body trembled. The intensity of the encounter left me exhausted, emotionally and physically.

Yes. I spoke with Chico, and the communication was real. He was as lost as I was. Confusion and sorrow mirrored back at me from across the void. We were both wounded, both bewildered, both desperate for answers that would not come immediately.

The encounter left me sleepless, haunted by questions I couldn't answer. I stayed awake, crying silently in the darkness. At home, with my mother, the woman who had caused my family so much pain, I struggled to voice my anguish. Words were difficult, my mouth still wired shut, but I had to speak. I called my sister, attempting to articulate the weight pressing down on me. I did not speak of my grandmother; our relationship was nonexistent, and the audacity of her interference had long since soured our bond. My mother and sister, I realized, were unavoidable, and so I tried to navigate the fractured family I had been left with.

Despite my pain, I forced myself to care for my children. I cooked, cleaned, and tended to their needs.

My mother, behind on rent because of me, grew frustrated with my efforts to regain independence. But I could not falter. My children were my motivation. I pushed through exhaustion, dizziness, and the constant ache of grief.

Weeks passed. I began venturing out, first with my mother, eventually reclaiming some independence. I returned my children to school, just a block from the site of the shooting. It felt surreal—terrifying, almost—but I knew it was necessary. Their safety and education mattered more than my lingering fears. I maintained a low profile, navigating familiar streets that once held horror, but I was determined not to let fear dominate our lives.

Physically, progress came slowly. I weaned off the suction machine, learned to control my saliva, and gradually stood upright without assistance. My throat tube had been removed, leaving a small healing hole that I covered with a bandage. My mouth remained wired for months, each word a struggle through pain, but I persevered. An at-home nurse introduced me to a medical rinse—Chlorhexidine Gluconate Oral Rinse—which allowed me to clean around the wires and manage odor.

Simple acts like brushing my teeth, which I had once taken for granted, became victories of their own.

After more than a month in my mother's small studio, I had regained enough strength and independence to move forward. My face remained swollen, my body bruised and scarred, but I carried myself proudly. I was alive. I had survived. I had my children.

I returned to the scene of the crime once or twice—not seeking closure, but seeking a connection, a moment to honor Chico's memory. Answers were elusive, but the act of returning felt necessary. Through it all, I did not realize it at the time, but God's presence had guided me, carrying me through the darkness, one agonizing step at a time.

I had been through the abyss. I had seen the other side, touched grief, felt the sting of loss, and survived. And through it all, I was still here.

Chapter 14: Leaving Chicago

The time had come to leave Chicago behind. The South Side, once a place I called home, had become, in my mind, a landscape of despair. The abandoned buildings, the people loitering on almost every corner, the young men succumbing to drugs, and the constant echo of sirens—all of it was suffocating. Brothers killing brothers, neighbors ignoring one another, lives cut short in the blink of an eye—it was sickening yet normalized. I had grown accustomed to it, living in it for so long that it had become my baseline, my "normal." But now, with the weight of reality pressing on me, I could no longer ignore the truth: if I stayed, my children would grow up seeing this chaos as ordinary.

For years, I had been blind to the larger world beyond my immediate surroundings. I had lived in a box—a box of contentment, of barely scraping by, of not knowing better. I had gone to college and worked hard after high school, but life, with its twists, detours, and having children, had slowed me down. I had sought love in all the wrong places, failing to nurture the one place that mattered most: my own heart and the love of my Creator. Now, that ignorance could no longer shelter me. It was time to break free.

East Troy, Wisconsin, became our new beginning. The change was jarring. For a city girl like me, a town defined by farms, rolling green pastures, and quiet streets felt almost surreal. When I left the hospital, my family had already moved my belongings into storage. On moving day, they repacked everything, and for two hours we drove to my new home—a small, low-income apartment in a quiet complex that promised peace I had never known. The rent was zero until I could find work, a blessing that felt almost unimaginable after years of financial struggle. For the first time in my life, I felt the faint glimmer of freedom and security.

In early to mid-April 2016, we settled into our new apartment. The children were ecstatic, discovering a backyard that seemed to stretch endlessly, where they could run freely and laugh without fear. The complex itself was filled with single mothers like me, a few couples, and some older residents who required assistance. A small park and a grocery store were within walking distance, but otherwise, everything needed was just a short drive away. There were no corner loiterers, no beggars pressing for change—just peace, and for the first time, it was ours.

My younger sister lived in a nearby town. She had secured her own low-income housing and guided me through the process of finding mine. She had her own struggles as a single mother, and her partner had chosen not to relocate. Even so, we were just fifteen minutes apart—a small comfort in this new chapter. Unfortunately, her stay was short-lived; she returned to Chicago to address her family responsibilities, leaving me to navigate this new life largely on my own.

I applied for Social Security benefits for Kaniya and Eman. Their father had been employed, so that meant they could receive them. Jeremiah's father contributed what he could, and though our communication was limited, that small consistency helped. When the benefits were approved, I finally had some steady income to sustain us while I continued to heal, both physically and emotionally.

Yet the greatest challenge remained: my face. I was still confined to a liquid diet and making slow progress. Every few weeks, I drove back to Chicago for follow-ups with Dr. Sinha and his team, who had painstakingly reconstructed my face and wired my jaw shut. The journey was long and taxing, but necessary. The state of Illinois, through Crime Victims Assistance, covered the majority of my medical expenses. Many of my doctors even worked with me from sheer kindness, never asking for payment personally, despite the complexities of my surgeries and recovery. The compassion they showed me—Dr. Sinha, his wife, the Oral and Maxillofacial Surgery team, and countless others were humbling. I cried as I left their offices, overwhelmed with gratitude. No amount of money could repay the human kindness I had received. These were angels in white coats, saving not just my face, but my future.

Life in East Troy was quiet, almost painfully so. There were days when the stillness bored me, when the contrast between this town and the chaos I had left behind felt surreal. But within the calm, the trauma of my recent past began to gnaw at me. I never sought formal treatment for what I was experiencing, but I knew, deep down, that I was wrestling with depression, paranoia, and the lingering shock of surviving a shooting. Nightmares plagued me—visions of young men in hoodies, guns drawn, stalking my children and me. Socializing felt impossible; I avoided neighbors, preferring the solitude of my apartment, though the loneliness weighed heavily.

Caring for three children on my own was both my anchor and my trial. Every day, I confronted my grief, fought back tears, and held them close while whispering, "Daddy is okay, and everything will be alright." Even as I said these words, I could not believe them myself. The pain and emptiness inside me were constant companions, yet somehow, I managed. Shockingly, I discovered a strength I had never known I possessed. Every day was a step forward, a small victory in a life that had been upended.

Our routines slowly reformed. The children attended school, their small worlds returning to order, while I remained at home, still unable to work. We lived on a monthly check, modest but sufficient. My children had what they needed, and I clung to that, even as I mourned the father who would never return.

Then, finally, the day arrived for my mouth to be opened—my first real taste of freedom in nearly three months. It was set for just after Mother's Day in May. I had been living on liquids, subsisting on milkshakes, smoothies, and soups, and now I would taste real food again. The drive to my appointment took two hours, but I welcomed it. I was nervous, eager, and almost giddy at the thought of chewing, swallowing, and reclaiming my body.

The procedure itself was brief, yet transformative. A cut to one wire that kept my mouth closed was finally split and the prison in my mouth lifted. My bottom teeth, still greatly misaligned, felt alien, yet the liberation was overwhelming. I returned home, driving through the countryside with anticipation, thinking about the first bite I would take. My cousin had prepared a plate of her soul food the day before—a feast I had been dreaming about for weeks. Macaroni and cheese, cornbread, chicken, spaghetti... each bite felt like a reclamation of life. My mouth was sore, my teeth sensitive, steel wires still held together fragile places, yet I ate with abandon. For the first time in months, I felt nourished, whole, and renewed.

Brushing my teeth became an act of both care and reverence. I could now reach the back, clean my tongue, and navigate the intricate wires and screws with patience. My mouth, a cage for so long, reminded me of the pain I had endured—but also of the resilience I had discovered within myself. I had survived, against all odds, and here I was, tasting life again, savoring each moment with a gratitude I could not fully articulate.

Chapter 15: A Name to That Face & Digging Deeper

Moving forward, I had to adapt to an entirely new rhythm of life—one defined by vigilance, trauma, and the relentless beat of survival. Every day was a tightrope walk: caring for my children, adjusting to a foreign town, managing the haunting pain in my face, and confronting the lingering shadow of that fateful day. Life in another state was calmer, yes, but a gnawing emptiness persisted, a silent, screaming echo that I could not name at first. Something was unfinished. Something had to be done. The person who had shattered my family, who had stolen my love and terrorized my children, had not yet faced justice—and my soul could not rest.

One afternoon, I found myself at the library with my children. They were small, innocent, and unaware of the evil that had invaded our lives. Kaniya and Jeremiah sat cross-legged in the children's section, flipping through books with intense concentration, while little Eman bounced in a chair next to me, clutching his favorite picture book. My heart ached. They were here without a father, without the man who had been their protector, their rock, and my partner in life. And yet, in the calm of that library, the memory of that day came rushing back—the bullets, the screams, the chaos, the smoke of gunfire still clinging to my mind like a curse.

A sudden thought struck me like a bolt of lightning: a flier. A tangible way to reach someone—anyone—who might help identify the monster who had ripped my life apart. Trembling, I slipped onto the computer next to my children and began typing. Each word was a prayer, each sentence a plea for justice. I begged, pleaded, almost screamed into the digital void: someone, anyone, please help me. I included a separate phone number, the detective's contact information, and my trembling hope that this small act might lead to answers.

That weekend, I made the pilgrimage back to Chicago. Driving past streets I had tried desperately to forget, I returned to the crime scene—the place where everything I had loved had been ripped from me. The memories hit with a force so intense I could barely breathe. My chest tightened, my stomach twisted. But I pressed on, slipping fliers under doors, tucking them under windshield wipers, leaving them where someone might see.

That night, I promised myself I would do everything in my power to catch this monster. Every waking moment would be devoted to bringing him to justice.

And then, it happened. My phone rang. The text, the call—it was simultaneous. I froze, my body betraying me. My knees gave way, and I collapsed onto the closed toilet seat, sobbing uncontrollably. Less than six months after the attack, I now had it: the name of the man who had shot me, shot at my children, and stolen Chico from us forever. Alongside the name came a photograph from his Facebook profile. His face stared back at me, slightly younger, the hat shadowing his features, yet unmistakable. My hands shook, my body quivering like a leaf in a storm. Tears poured freely as I stared at the man who had brought my world to its knees.

The one who had sent me the photo had obtained my number through Chico's family. I would never forget that moment of recognition. I had seen many false leads before. I remembered when Chico's aunt had sent me a picture, asking if it was him. I had stared at the photo, shaking my head, whispering, "No. Not him." Something deep in me knew. The eyes—the eyes of my attacker—were burned into my memory. When he had emerged from that alleyway, bullets flying, time had slowed. I had looked into his eyes, and I had seen pure evil. My mind had taken a mental photograph that no years, no distance, could erase.

Eyes are everything. When someone steps into your life, whether as a friend, lover, or enemy, the first connection is through the eyes. And his eyes—they were frozen in darkness, a void that swallowed light and hope. I had stared into that abyss for seconds that stretched into eternity. The world had stopped, and in that frozen moment, I had seen the soul of the man who sought to destroy us.

With the name now in hand, I contacted the detectives. I was trembling with a mixture of joy, grief, and rage. Finally, there was a tangible path forward. A single clue, a single piece of the puzzle, but enough to ignite hope. I spent hours combing through social media, meticulously scanning photographs, posts, and associations. His own page revealed little, but his circle—a web of friends, associates, and enablers—was an open window into a culture of chaos. Guns, gang signs, violence, and mockery of life itself. Women and men alike flaunted weapons, posted taunts, laughed at death. I was horrified. Their posts were careless, brazen, ignorant—a portrait of a community consumed by its own destruction.

I saw it all—the cryptic emojis, the smirks, the sunglasses over grins, the subtle codes that marked them as a gang. They were laughing about February 27, 2016, mocking the day that had nearly destroyed me. And there, among the group photos, I saw him again. Slightly younger, different hoodie, yet unmistakable. The posture, the stance, the very essence of the man—the same as that day—frozen in a photograph. His hand raised in the position of a gun, the embodiment of the violence he had enacted.

I could close my eyes, and I was transported back to that moment. The cold air biting my face, the laughter of my children, the deafening sound of gunfire. I could feel the fear, the adrenaline, the frozen terror as time had slowed. The clarity was unbearable, but it was also a blessing. This man—the one who had almost destroyed us—was finally identified. And I had God's providence guiding me to the truth.

This was no longer abstract. This was real. This was him. My flier, my outreach, my relentless pursuit—it had not been in vain. Every tear, every sleepless night, every moment of despair had led to this. I now had a name to that face, a path forward, and a purpose that burned hotter than any fear: justice.

But the fight was far from over. I could feel it in my bones. The world would not simply hand justice over, and the path ahead was riddled with obstacles. The darkness of that day still lingered, the echo of gunfire still haunted my nights, and the pain in my heart still throbbed with every memory. Yet for the first time, I felt a measure of control. I was no longer completely at the mercy of fate. I had a direction, a mission, and the unyielding determination to see it through.

And as I held my children close that night, whispering promises of safety and strength, I knew one thing with certainty: I would not rest until justice was served. For Chico. For my children. For the woman who had survived against all odds. I had found the monster—and now, I would see him face the consequences of his actions.

Chapter 16:
Moving Again & Going Back to School

2016 was a year defined by movement, both physical and emotional. In the span of a few months, I moved twice—first to a state far from everything I knew, then again, closer to Chicago, where the ghosts of our past still lurked in the shadows. I was young, exhausted, and depressed, teetering on the edge of my own sanity. Every weekend, I foolishly drove back and forth, four hours each trip, just to visit friends and family, trying to breathe in a sense of normalcy while the walls of my mind closed in around me.

Life outside my home seemed effortless for everyone else. Friends laughed, traveled, met new people, and lived their best years with an ease I could barely recognize. And there I was, sitting in my quiet living room, my children tugging at my sleeves, begging me to come outside and play. My face was still healing, swollen and crooked, my teeth ensnared in metal wires, and a long scar ran from under my bottom lip across my chin. I smiled at them, but the smile didn't reach my eyes. I felt trapped in my own body, in my own life. I watched them run, their laughter slicing through my despair like sunlight through storm clouds. That mattered, yes, but inside, I was still dying a little each day.

For months, I forced myself to exist in two worlds: the one my children lived in, full of play and joy, and the one I inhabited, thick with grief, rage, and the echo of gunfire. Yet, slowly, I began to change. At first, I obsessed over my face, my wires, the scar that made me feel unworthy of the life everyone else seemed to enjoy. But eventually, I realized that no one around me cared how I looked—my friends, my family, my children—they didn't see my flaws. Only I did. And in that realization, a small seed of freedom took root.

By the end of the year, I moved closer to Chicago—not for convenience alone, but because my recovery demanded it. My surgeries were not finished; my mouth and chin required monitoring almost weekly. I needed to be close to my doctors, to have support readily available. And I wanted to try school again, hoping to reclaim the part of myself I had abandoned—

the part of me that still dreamed, that still sought knowledge and growth.

As crazy as it sounds, I needed a fresh start, a place that could help me smile again and reconnect with the life I wanted—not just survive, but live. I began looking for apartments closer to the city, closer to opportunity, closer to everything I had sacrificed for survival.

It was a bold, somewhat reckless decision. I gave up a low-income haven for stability, ready to trade security for proximity. Four hours of driving each weekend had taken a toll; my children sometimes missed school when appointments ran long. The thought of being near the schools, daycares, and support systems felt liberating. I would live off the children's income for a while until I found work, and although it felt selfish, I convinced myself it was necessary. I needed to breathe. I needed to reclaim some part of myself.

Our new neighborhood was diverse and vibrant. The children attended excellent schools, daycare was wonderful for Eman, and I finally had a semblance of peace. The community wasn't perfect—hood boys still passed through occasionally—but the police presence had increased, and the corner store notorious for illegal activity had been shut down. Slowly, I felt the grip of fear loosen.

Life started to feel... possible. I enrolled in school again, taking only three courses at first to ease myself back into academic life. I purchased a laptop from a pawn shop and a cheap printer from a local department store and established a nightly routine of studying after the children fell asleep. The world of knowledge wrapped around me, filling the void that trauma had carved inside me. Slowly, my confidence returned. I raised my hand in class, answered questions, and participated in discussions—my mind awakened after months of stagnation. The metal in my mouth no longer held me back. I was present in the world, learning, surviving, and even starting to thrive.

But the fire of justice still burned deep. One night, as I finished my homework, I made a new batch of flyers. This time, I included a family photo—Chico, the children, and me. Maybe someone out there would see it and feel compelled to act. Months had passed since the initial flyers were distributed, and the case had stalled. But I refused to let it die. The shooter needed to know I was still here. I would not rest.

About a week or two later, I returned to the scene of Chico's final moments. The air was thick with memory—the chill of that February day, the sharp tang of gunpowder lingering in my mind, the echo of my children's screams. I placed twenty flyers under doors, tucked some under windshield wipers, praying that someone, anyone, would feel the weight of our loss and come forward. My heart pounded. My hands shook. But I left with hope, small but resolute, knowing that every act, no matter how minor it seemed, was a step toward justice.

Even as I rebuilt my life, the private battles raged on. At night, alone in my apartment, I would stare into the mirror, tracing the scar across my chin, touching the metal still in my mouth, and crying. I would sift through photos of Chico, our children, and me, letting grief pour from me in torrents until my soul felt hollow. And then, somehow, I would rise. I would brush my teeth, prepare breakfast for my children, and step out into the world with a smile. This duality—mourning and living—was the strange gift God had given me: the ability to feel every ounce of sorrow and still keep moving forward.

On December 14, 2016, I faced a milestone in my recovery: the removal of every wire, screw, and band from my mouth—ten long, excruciating months of being trapped in metal. My mother came to drive me, and I arrived at Dr. Sinha's office with trembling anticipation. Laughing gas and numbing injections offered little relief against the sheer agony of what was to come. Each cut of wire, each twist of the screwdriver unscrewing the metal holding my teeth in place, sent torrents of pain racing through my body—pain far surpassing labor or childbirth.

Tears streamed uncontrollably as I screamed, begging for it to stop. The assistants looked at me as though I had lost my mind, instructing me to breathe, to calm down, to endure. And I did, as best I could, though my soul was raw and trembling. My thoughts wandered back to that day, to the man who had put me here, to the life I had almost lost. And still, when I left the office, bloodied, exhausted, yet alive, I thanked the team for their care and perseverance. This place would become a second home, my sanctuary for recovery, my fortress of healing.

School became my lifeline. My three courses were challenging, but they reignited the spark of purpose inside me. Each night, after my children slept, I studied diligently, completing assignments, writing papers, and immersing myself in knowledge. The world of learning became my anchor, reminding me that I was more than my trauma, more than my scars, more than my past.

Kashe's 24th birthday at Navy Pier in Chicago, Illinois.
Age: Kashe 24, Chico 25
Fun Fact: Kashe met Chico when she was 12.

Chico and Kaniya. (2014)

Chico and Eman. (2015)

FAITH STRONGER THAN BULLETS | 91

Chico pictured here with his stepson Jeremiah, whom he loved and Kaniya in the back, picking up a toy she dropped.

The vehicle Kashe was robbed in.

Newspaper clipping on the shooting aftermath. (August 2022)

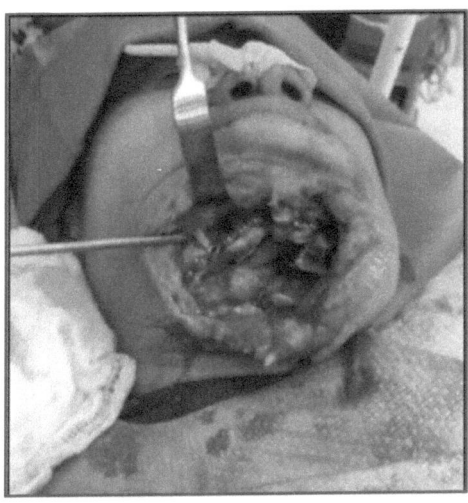

Kashe during surgery.

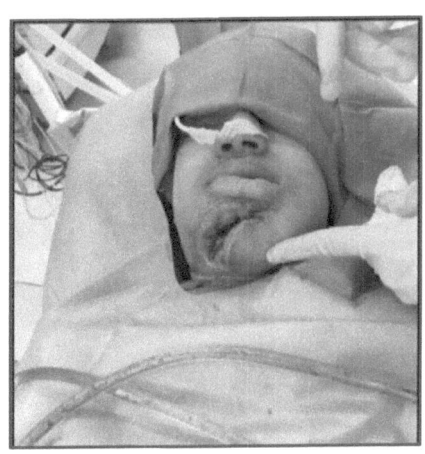

Kashe during surgery.

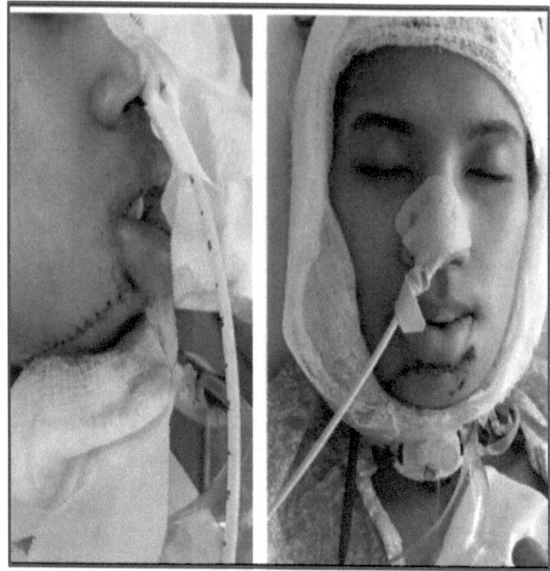

Kashe after surgery.

Kashe's dental prosthetic.

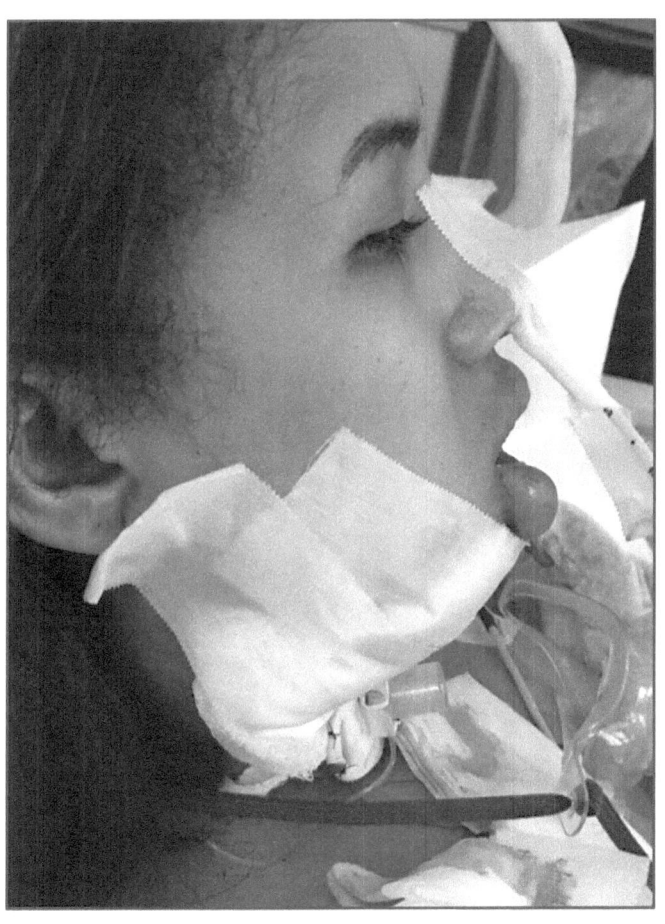

Kashe after surgery.

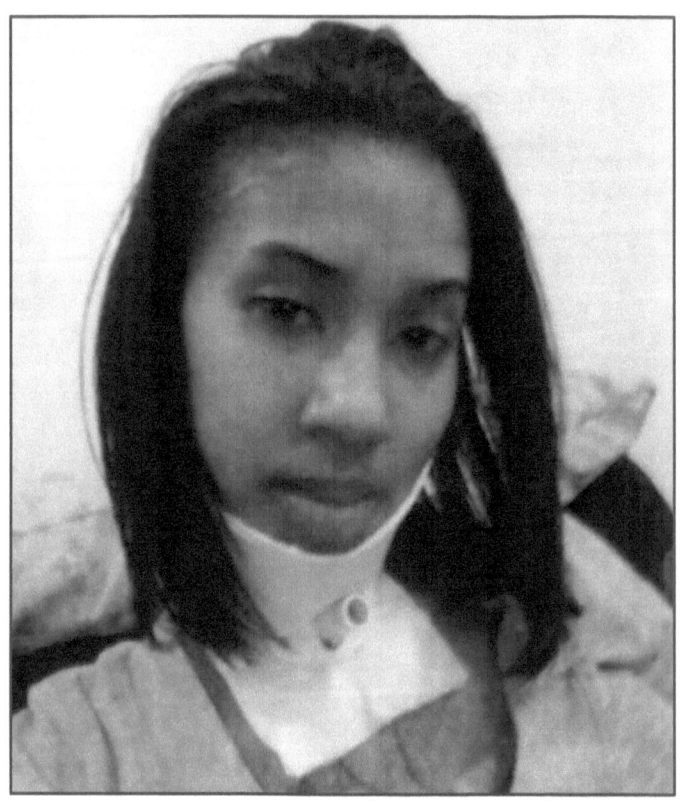

Kashe two weeks after surgery with trach tube.

Kashe reflecting after leaving home with gratitude in her heart—trusting the road ahead is worth the distance behind her.

Kaniya, Jeremiah, Eman, and Kashe.

Chapter 17:
The Start Of Many Court Dates

A year had passed since that fateful day, yet the memory of it remained as sharp as the day it happened. Every sound, every shadow, every scream from my children reminded me of what was lost. And now, on April 27, 2017, exactly one year and two months after the man who tried to erase our lives had pulled the trigger, everything had shifted. He was finally being held accountable.

Authorities came to his home quietly, arresting him while he went about his ordinary life, unaware that the world he had upended was now closing in on him. The detective who called me that day said, "He was quiet the whole ride, with a strange, blank look on his face." Quiet—but not hidden. Soon, his face—the face I would never forget—would confront the law. And me.

I cried as the call ended, tears flowing for the lost time, for the fear in my children's eyes, for the lives that had almost been taken and the one taken. A strange mix of relief and anticipation coursed through me. I had imagined this moment countless times, dreaming of the day justice would intersect with reality. Yet nothing had prepared me for how raw it would feel to see him in custody, the man who had tried to snuff out the lives of my family and me.

I would soon have to visit the precinct where he was being held and identify him in a line-up. I wouldn't be alone—Chris, Chico's closest friend, said that he would support me. Chris had become family to us, a constant presence in our lives after the shooting. He had shared our grief, lived with us for a short time, and comforted my children as if they were his own. He himself was no stranger to violence. Sometime after our shooting, Chris had been shot on the South Side, left for dead after complying with his attackers' demands. One bullet had nearly claimed his life, and yet he had survived. Hearing him recount his story made my own survival feel both miraculous and burdened with responsibility. Lady B also got shot while getting food on the Southside. She too survived! We were all survivors, and now we had a mission: justice.

That day arrived. I remember the night before, lying awake, heart pounding, wondering how I would handle seeing him again. My stomach was twisted into knots, and a weight pressed against my chest that sleep could not lift. I clutched my children close that night, reminding myself silently that I had to be strong—not just for them, but for the memory of Chico and the future of justice.

When we arrived at the precinct, the air was thick with anticipation. The offender, now a few feet from me, escorted by officers, and I could feel the electricity of the moment coil tight in my chest.

Seeing him again since that day he shot us hurt my soul. I picked him out in a previous lineup, but this was gut-wrenching. The glass between us did little to lessen the impact. My eyes locked on him, and I could see that he was not the same man. Gone was the bold, unshakable figure who had held a gun to my world. Now he swayed nervously, unable to remain still. His eyes darted downward as if avoiding contact, yet I could feel the tension radiating from him. His hair was matted, his clothes disheveled, and he looked years older than the day he tried to steal our lives.

Even behind glass, his presence was suffocating. I could feel my pulse quicken, my throat tighten, and the flood of memories came crashing back: the roar of the gunfire, the screams of my children, the split-second decisions that kept us alive. The trauma of that day intertwined with the anticipation of justice—it was almost too much to bear. But I stayed strong. For my children, myself, and for Chico.

Over the next several months, I would attend multiple court dates, each one a trial of endurance, patience, and emotional fortitude. Each one wasn't a long procedure, but even seeing him walk in and out as the case got continued time after time was hard. Each session opened wounds that were only partially healed, forcing me to relive the shooting over and over.

Outside the courtroom, I often reflected on the surreal nature of the proceedings. I would sit in my car, heart pounding, replaying each moment over and over. I thought about Chico, about the life we had shared, and the future he had been robbed of. I thought about my children, and how each court date reminded them that the world could be both cruel and just. And I thought about myself—how much strength, courage, and resilience I had unearthed simply by surviving and insisting that the world see the truth.

Chris remained a constant presence, his own pain woven into every story he shared. He had been robbed, shot, and left for dead, yet he never wavered in supporting me. I often caught him staring at the offender, eyes narrowed, a mix of anger, sorrow, and disbelief. He had lost Chico, too, and I understood that our collective grief fueled the determination in the courtroom. We were united in purpose, driven by the unrelenting need for justice.

Every court date was exhausting, both mentally and emotionally. Yet each session reinforced a truth I had clung to since the shooting: I had survived. My children had survived. And no matter how long the judicial system took, justice was not only possible—it was inevitable.

Chapter 18: Being Tested

Time passed, and life continued moving in strange, uneven rhythms. On the surface, I still enjoyed moments with my family and friends, but underneath, a quiet loneliness had settled in—a solitude I couldn't escape. I began withdrawing, finding comfort in silence, in prayer, and in the pages of the Bible. I opened Genesis, hoping to find clarity, guidance, a roadmap to understanding life and suffering.

But the language was foreign, distant. Names blurred together like echoes of people I would never meet. Generations of sons and daughters slipped past me, and I became frustrated. I wanted to *understand*, not just skim over verses. I wanted God to be real, tangible, present every day. But I didn't know how to reach Him. I didn't know how to speak in a way that mattered, in a way that would make my heart feel His presence. I wasn't praying "wrongly," exactly—but I was fumbling in the dark, yearning for guidance I couldn't yet grasp.

I had lived a lifetime of pain before that day—the day my children and I were shot in a car, my love stolen from me in an instant. And now, here I was, still standing, still breathing, trying to reconcile survival with devastation. I thought of Job, the man who lost everything yet never wavered in his faith. I saw myself in him—not in the righteousness, but in the confusion, the anguish, the unanswered questions. I, too, had cried out to God, "Why us? Why me? Why my children?" And like Job, I had no answers, only the raw, gnawing presence of suffering.

I questioned everything. Was I cursed? Had I done something to deserve this? Had my life been a series of missteps and misfortunes that had led me to this broken, hollow place? The answers didn't come. I only had the moments of survival, the quiet miracle that my children and I were still alive. And in those moments, the faint spark of faith began to flicker. Somehow, in the wreckage of my life, God had kept us alive.

Healing was a slow, torturous process. Even months after the shooting, my body was a battlefield. August 30, 2017—another date etched in my memory—marked my second surgery on my jaw. The first surgery had tried to reconstruct what bullets had shattered; this second one would test me even further. My mandible—the lower jawbone—hadn't healed correctly. Bones in my face had been obliterated, shattered beyond recognition. Imagine the lower half of your face reduced to fragments, wires and screws holding what remained together, skin pulled tight over raw bone. The thought alone made me dizzy.

I had to relive every detail. X-rays, examinations, and planning sessions. Dr. Sinha explained that bone from my hip might be needed to rebuild my face. My stomach turned. The first time had been unbearable, but now—knowing what was coming—fear wrapped around me like chains. Stitches. Wires. Screws. Pain. Days in Christ Hospital. Swelling, bleeding, the inability to eat, to speak normally. I had survived bullets, but the surgical tables became their own kind of battlefield.

The day of surgery, I remember lying there, staring at the ceiling, listening to the hum of the machines and the quiet steps of the nurses. My mind raced: *Will my lip drop? Will my face ever look like mine again? Will I be able to smile without crying?*

Pain wasn't the only enemy—I was fighting the disfigurement, the reality that my body would bear this horror forever. Every scar, every crooked tooth was a constant reminder of the night that tried to erase my life.

I woke up swollen, bruised, my mouth wired with partial reconstruction, four bottom teeth gone. I had lost a part of myself that I didn't even realize I cherished—the teeth that framed my smile, the subtle curves that made me feel human. Suddenly, everyday acts became trials. Eating. Speaking.

Looking in a mirror. My reflection became a stranger, a face I barely recognized, a person who had survived something horrific but was paying the price in ways no one could see.

Going outside was terrifying. I covered my mouth, avoided eye contact, and felt invisible shame weighing down every step. People didn't know, couldn't see the scars under the skin, but I did. I felt ugliness in a way that cut deeper than any bullet ever could. When men approached, I politely declined, hiding behind my hand, retreating from connection. My confidence, once taken for granted, had been fractured, scattered across hospital beds and surgical tables.

And yet, through it all, I survived. My faith, fragile and flickering, began to root itself in the small victories: waking up, taking care of my children, completing schoolwork, and enduring hospital stays. I began to pray—not just asking for relief, but asking for strength. *God, let me keep going. Let me survive this pain. Let me be here for my children. Let me not lose myself.*

By February 13, 2018, I received partial dentures to replace my missing teeth. It was a small victory, yet monumental. Four teeth, sculpted to fit perfectly into my surgically reconstructed gums. At first, they felt alien in my mouth, awkward and unnatural. I had to adjust, to remember to place them in before leaving the house, to navigate a world that stared unknowingly at my imperfections. On that first day walking out with them, I felt a strange mix of shame and triumph—this was my new reality, my second chance at a semblance of normalcy.

Every day, I was tested—by my reflection, by strangers' eyes, by my own inner doubts. But each day, I also learned resilience, courage, and acceptance. I had survived bullets and blood, disfigurement and surgeries, grief and despair. I had faced the reality of a world that could be cruel and emerged alive, still learning, still striving, still human.

Through it all, I clung to God. Slowly, imperfectly, I began to understand that survival was not just about being alive—it was about *being present*, about finding purpose in the ruins. My children needed me. My life had meaning. And despite the scars—inside and out—I would continue moving forward, one difficult, painful, miraculous day at a time.

Chapter 19:
A Visit From An Evil Entity

October 1, 2018, started like any other day—or so I thought. I lay in bed as the quiet hum of the morning settled over the house. I was off work, yet my alarm had been set for six a.m., though I woke well before it rang. I lingered under the covers, savoring a few stolen moments of rest before facing the day, before having to rouse my children from slumber and prepare them for school and daycare.

Then it began.

A presence. A feeling of eyes watching me from the darkness. At first, it was subtle, like a shadow brushing the edges of consciousness. But soon, the atmosphere thickened. The air around me vibrated, almost alive with something *not of this world*. I tried to shake it off, telling myself it was fatigue, imagination, the remnants of dreams I barely remembered.

Then came the voices.

Soft, almost melodic, but urgent, insistent:

Get up... and run!

Get up and run!

My eyes fully opened, heart pounding. What? Who? Why run? My mind raced, struggling to process what I was hearing. The voices seemed angelic, pleading, yet trembling with the weight of something enormous and unseen.

Before I could move, before I could even fully comprehend the warning, I felt it. *Hands*. Cold, unnatural, pressing against my neck and arm, holding me down with a force I could not resist. Though I couldn't turn my head, my eyes wide but half-blinded, and there it was—or, rather, I *saw it*. Not in a way that made sense physically, but spiritually. I could see it, though I could not see it. A shadow, a darkness, a presence of absolute evil.

It hovered near my right ear, just behind the back of my head, but the sensation was all-encompassing, as if it surrounded me completely. Its form was blacker than midnight, darker than shadow itself—like black licorice that had somehow grown a body, a soul, a consciousness. A living nightmare given shape. Its voice hissed directly into my ear, a serpentine whisper full of malice:

GET UP… AND GO GET YOUR KIDDDDSSSSSS!

My heart froze. My body trembled. I wanted to scream, but no sound emerged. I wanted to move, but my muscles refused. My eyes were open, yet everything felt warped, unreal. I was paralyzed, trapped in a nightmare that had somehow spilled into the real world.

And then, instinctively, I called His name. Jesus. *Jesus. Jesus. Jesus.* Over and over in my mind, a lifeline to the One I had been learning to trust. Slowly, ever so slowly, I felt the grip loosen. The presence wavered, as if recognizing the power of the name I invoked. My body shuddered violently, and finally, I could move again. I sprang from the bed, lungs gasping, and ran.

I needed to see my children. I needed to make sure they were safe. The panic clawed at me as I rushed through the hall, first to my son's room—empty. Then the dining area, the kitchen—still empty. And finally, I found them: all of my children, huddled together in Kaniya's bed, sleeping peacefully. Relief and terror collided in my chest. The entity had been here—so close to *them*. The thought sent icy shivers down my spine.

I stumbled to the kitchen sink, gagging violently. My body convulsed, as though it were expelling some foreign presence. Air burned my lungs; something had tried to force its way through me. I bent over, heaving, and then I felt it leave. A weight lifted, and I shivered violently, broken and trembling, tears streaming down my face.

I collapsed at the dining room table, sobbing, shaking, trying to reconcile what had just happened. My home—my sanctuary—had been invaded. By what? By whom? A demonic presence, tangible, real, and terrifying. I could feel it still, lingering behind me, a whisper in my spine, a shadow over my soul.

I reached for my phone and called my uncle, my pastor, my guide in matters of faith. I needed someone who understood the unseen world, someone who could help me make sense of what I had experienced. I explained everything, voice trembling, words tumbling out in disjointed bursts. He listened patiently, then spoke with clarity and authority that steadied my soul: *The devil is trying to stop you, Kashe. He is trying to scare you, slow you down, and make you doubt yourself. He knows you are growing in wisdom, growing in faith, moving toward success and purpose.*

He knows that you are headed toward God, toward your calling, and he will fight every step of the way. Stand firm. Do not fear him.

Tears streamed freely as I listened. Every word resonated. He was right. The attack wasn't random—it was targeted. I had been building, healing, growing, stepping closer to God and to the life I had been promised. And now, this entity had come to intimidate me, to make me falter, to instill fear.

I thought about the path I had walked since that shooting two years prior. Every moment had been a fight: surgeries, recovery, raising children alone, attending school, beginning my writing journey. I had survived bullets, survived grief, survived disfigurement. I had clawed my way back into life, and yet here was this darkness, trying to undo everything.

I drew a deep, steadying breath. My children were safe. My faith, though still growing, was real. I remembered the lessons of perseverance, of trusting God even in fear, of standing firm when all else threatens to crumble. I stood, resolute, and spoke aloud for the first time: *You are not welcome in this house. You will not touch my children. You will not win. My God will protect us, and we will forever belong to Him.*

I felt a surge of power, a lightness, a clarity. The entity had been confronted. Its influence, though lingering in the shadows of memory, was powerless in the face of faith. I got my children ready, walked them out the door, and for the first time that morning, breathed freely again.

Even now, as I write this, the memory is sharp, vivid, terrifying—but also empowering. God works in ways we cannot always see. He sent angels to warn me, to protect me, to remind me that my path was not without guidance. And in that moment, I understood something profound: the darkness will always try to stop those who are moving forward, but light, faith, and determination will always prevail.

October 1, 2018, was not just a day of fear—it was a day of affirmation. I had been tested. I had faced evil, and I had stood. I was alive, my children were safe, and my faith had grown stronger. Nothing—neither darkness, nor violence, nor fear—could break what God had promised me.

Chapter 20:
Did I Just Have Another Gun Pointed At Me?

I kept seeing a gun. Not in my hands. Not in someone else's. But in my mind. A vivid image that haunted me whenever I went in my garage. There was a particular spot in the backyard, a narrow patch I passed daily on my way in and out. And there it was: always in that spot, always the same gun, floating, unyielding. Every time I glimpsed it, I froze mid-step, my stomach twisting in knots.

"What in the hell?" I muttered to myself, brushing it off as exhaustion or imagination, but the image refused to fade. Days passed, and the vision persisted. My heart would race every time I approached that spot, my pulse loud in my ears. My friends didn't understand. I couldn't explain. I had seen enough guns in my life to know the weight, the fear, the threat they carried. And this… this was a warning I didn't yet understand.

Then came the night of December 30th, 2018, sliding quietly into the first hours of New Year's Eve. I had been driving for Uber for just over a month, supplementing my income, working on my own terms. I liked the independence, the lack of a boss, the hours I could dictate. But late-night driving was a gamble. I was careful, usually stopping around nine p.m., listening to advice from my very first rider, a woman who warned me that staying out past dark as a young woman was asking for trouble. I had laughed it off then, but that night, I realized how naive I had been.

It was nearly four a.m. when I pulled off the expressway near my apartment. The streets were empty, the cold biting into my skin. Two young teens loitered at the bus stop near my garage, shadows against the dim glow of a single streetlamp. My garage was directly behind them. For a moment, I hesitated, considering turning around, but exhaustion outweighed caution. I had made good money, and I just wanted to collapse into my bed.

I didn't see them move. I didn't see them follow. I didn't know that the moment I swung my car into the garage entrance, they would then be right behind me.

I parked quickly, the engine ticking as it cooled, and stepped out. That's when I saw him—a young boy who I believe had a gun in his hand. It was one of those old and skinny types that could kill as easily as scare. His hood shadowed his face, but I saw his eyes—dark, determined, hungry for what wasn't his. My heart dropped to my stomach, cold dread consuming me.

"Hand over the keys," he said, the voice a mixture of adolescent bravado and danger.

I froze. A million thoughts collided in my mind. My kids. My life. My survival. All I could think to do was throw the keys at him, my hands trembling so violently I could barely let go. He caught them and, without hesitation, turned to get into the car, leaving me frozen in disbelief.

I ran.

Through the garage door, up my back doorsteps is the only place I could think to run. Fear sat in my chest like a physical weight, pressing down, suffocating. I collapsed on the back steps, tears streaming down my face.

My hands shook uncontrollably. My body had relived the shooting all over again—the helplessness, the terror, the "what if?" haunting every second.

I dialed 911, then my best friend, who lived across the hall and often watched my children while I worked. Her voice was a lifeline, grounding me, anchoring me back to reality. Minutes later, police arrived. My vehicle was gone, taken in seconds.

Nothing more than a material loss—but to me, it was a violation, another reminder of the fragility of life, of the randomness of violence, and of how quickly safety could be stripped away.

The next days were torture. Sleep became impossible. Every shadow, every creak in the floor, every sound outside my window made me jump. I barricaded doors, kept knives close, and refused to leave my home unless necessary. I was a mother, a protector, a survivor—but inside, I was fractured.

A couple of days later, the detective called. Fingerprints from the vehicle had been recovered. One boy would be arrested. Others would likely slip through the cracks. I felt anger, despair, and exhaustion all at once. My mind went back to that night—the fear, the adrenaline, the utter helplessness—and I wondered how so many young lives could be so reckless, so selfish, so willing to inflict harm for nothing.

Months passed, and eventually, in April 2019, the arrested boy appeared in court. I had to see him. Another courtroom, another exercise in confronting fear. The boy was taller than the one who had held me at gunpoint. His fingerprints had led to the arrest, but I couldn't be sure he was actually there at the time of the robbery. Still, there he sat, in front of me, shoulders slumped, eyes downcast. His grandfather sat in the row ahead, looking helpless and pained.

The courtroom was cold and impersonal, a stark contrast to the terror that had consumed me in my garage. I listened as the proceedings went on, feeling a strange mix of anger, sorrow, and pity. This boy had made choices that would shape the rest of his life, and here he was—caught, yet barely understanding the gravity of his actions.

The judge's ruling was light probation. "Unauthorized trespass to a vehicle." Not knowing whether he was there during the robbery or just hopped in later led to this light sentence. Overall, this one act caused trauma, fear, and psychological scars.

I looked at him one last time before leaving the courtroom. His yellowed, sorrow-filled eyes met mine. He lowered his head, shame washing over him in silence, like a child bowing before the weight of consequences he barely understood. It was a stark reminder that crime doesn't just hurt the victim—it destroys everyone connected to it. I left the courtroom with a sense of exhaustion, a hollow victory. And yet, I prayed for him.

In the midst of all this, I remembered God. I remembered how He had protected me, how He had spared my children and me once again.

I stood outside, breathing the cold air, and whispered a prayer: "Lord, thank You for keeping us alive. Thank you for guiding us through another night, another terror, another test. Help me to keep my heart strong, my mind clear, and my soul aligned with You."

I walked away from the courthouse, from the trial, and from the fear that had gripped me, realizing that while I could not control the actions of others, I could control my response. I could heal. I could protect. I could trust.

The events of that night, and the weeks that followed, left me scarred—but alive. And surviving, I realized, was a victory in itself. Every gun pointed at me, every dark shadow of darkness, every court date—it was all a test of faith, endurance, and resilience. And I had passed.

Because in the end, my life, my children, and my faith were mine. And no one—not the young boys, not the shooter, not the darkness—could take that away.

Chapter 21:
Go Home, Chico

In 2016, my family and I were shot execution-style, and we lost Dad. That day fractured everything, leaving scars no one could see but me. And then, in 2018, as if life wanted to remind me of its cruel unpredictability, I was robbed at gunpoint. Mentally, emotionally, spiritually—I felt set back again. Each day, I tried to rebuild. Each day, I tried to breathe. But the memories replayed relentlessly, like a broken record that no therapy could fully silence.

Kaniya, my sweet angel, has had dreams of her father visiting her shortly after his passing. It was comforting to see that she could process some of her grief in her sleep. At that time, she was seeing an excellent therapist, someone Kaniya adored and trusted. She would talk about their sessions, her little face lighting up, saying, "It's nice to talk about it, Mom." Months later, her therapist cleared her, deeming her mental state stable. From my perspective, Kaniya was flourishing. We were all surviving. Thriving, even. Because we had each other, we were enough.

Today, Kaniya still remembers her father, but in a way that is so profoundly different than I expected. She rarely speaks of him with sorrow. When she does, it is always about his laugh, his kindness, or the moments they shared. For someone her age—and considering the trauma she witnessed—it's nothing short of remarkable. She has chosen, consciously or unconsciously, to anchor herself in God. That decision has softened the weight of grief and allowed her light to shine unshaken. Even as a child, Kaniya possessed a maturity beyond her years. I remember looking at her when she was about seven, noticing something I couldn't yet name: a quiet anointing, a spiritual presence.

One afternoon, I asked her gently, "Baby, you know you've been through things no child should ever have to face. You were there when your dad passed, and you've seen and felt pain that I can't even imagine. Are you really okay?"

She looked up at me, eyes like his, shimmering with wisdom beyond her years. "Ma, my daddy is with God, and God is amazing. I'm okay. Yes, I sometimes cry because I miss him, but God left you here to love me and take care of me. I love God. And I love my daddy."

Tears fell freely down my cheeks as I listened. Even now, writing these words, I weep because I see clearly: I had an angel standing before me, guiding me, helping me stay afloat. "God saved you so you could still love me and take care of me," Kaniya had said. And He did. And He saved her, too, so that she could save me.

We all think of Chico—the way his smile lit a room, the way he cared, the way he loved fiercely. He was a man searching for himself, trying to navigate life after prison, trying to mend old wounds while facing new ones. Locked away for six and a half years, the trauma he carried was immense, and I suspect I only ever saw the surface. Chico was special. He could enter a room and make everyone feel lighter, brighter. But inside, he wrestled with demons I didn't yet understand.

Chico was born on August 26, 1989, and passed away on February 27, 2016. Twenty-six years young. Four children, three biological, one stepson—each one missing their father until he returned, only to leave them again far too soon. I watched him struggle, watched him fight battles I didn't yet know how to help with. He wanted to break generational curses. He wanted to be better.

And sometimes, he was. But other times, he took the easy road, the path that led to destruction, unaware of the consequences. Yet, through it all, he loved deeply. He laughed loudly. He tried.

Even after his passing, he lingered. Spiritually. Emotionally. Sometimes in my dreams, sometimes in those moments when the world seemed to quiet just enough for me to feel him nearby. After my first spiritual encounter with Chico during REM sleep, I never heard his voice again. I only saw his presence. It was heavy, sorrowful, unfinished. Chico was restless, tethered to this world by love and loss.

Years later, that presence returned in a particularly unsettling way. An ex-friend of mine brought a "Chucky Doll" into my apartment. It sat there, innocuous to the eye, but spiritually, it seemed to carry a weight. I felt it—darkness lurking, probing, testing. And in that same room, I could see Chico, protective and sorrowful, hovering near the bed where I slept. He touched my leg once, lightly, as if warning me or guiding me. At the foot of the bed, another darker entity loomed, watching. The atmosphere was suffocating.

I spoke to him through tears, my voice cracking. "Chico… is that you? Are you here?"

No answer came. His spirit lingered, unwilling to leave his children's side—or perhaps unwilling to leave me.

With a heart heavy but determined, I said the words that would finally release him: "Just… Go Home, Chico. I don't want to let you go—it kills me that you're gone, that I had to watch you die. Our children need you, even if you can't be here. My surgeries hurt, my heart hurts, but I will take care of them. I'll love them fiercely. I'll love you, always. But now, you go home. Find peace. Find your place in His Kingdom. Serve. Save yourself. So that one day, we may see you again. GO HOME."

Not long after, while sitting in that same room, my phone—my everyday companion—spoke in a voice I would never forget: "There is a ghost in your room." It used one of those assistant voices, an impossibility by human logic. I was in shock, flabbergasted. I called the friend who had brought the doll immediately. It was removed. I cleansed the space with sage—not because I fully believed, but because I needed to act, and that friend mentioned sage. Slowly, gradually, the oppressive weight lifted. The darkness receded. Chico's spirit departed. I now know it was because of that prayer and that doll leaving the house. Also, Kaniya foretelling what was to come and her assurance within it.

Finally, there was quiet. Peace. Closure.

I realized something profound in that moment: life will never stop testing you. Pain, loss, grief, trauma—they will try to claim your body, your mind, your soul. But you have a choice: to falter, or to rise. I chose to rise. Every time I wanted to give up, every time a shadow or a spirit tried to unsettle me, I remembered God. I remembered Chico. I remembered my children, my reason for breathing, my mission for surviving.

Little ole Kashe was alone in body, yes, but never alone in spirit. I could not see Him, could not touch Him, could not hear Him in the ordinary ways, but He was there. He sent guidance, sent protection, sent helpers in the most unlikely forms.

"Yea, though I walk through the valley of the shadow of death, I will fear no evil; for You are with me; Your rod and Your staff, they comfort me" (Psalm 23:4, NKJV).

And that day, in the quiet aftermath of spiritual battles, I understood—my strength wasn't mine alone. My courage, my love, my resilience—they were gifts. And my path? It was still being walked with divine purpose, with protection I could feel even when I could not see it.

I whispered into the silence, one last prayer for Chico: "Go home. Find rest. Be free. Until we meet again."

And for the first time in years, I believed he had.

Chapter 22:
The Lord Jesus Was In My Room

I'll never forget the call from the State's Attorney's Office: "We are finally going to trial."

The words landed like a gunshot inside my chest. My heart froze. I had been waiting for this moment for years—longer than I could count—and now it was here. I would face the man who had shattered my life, who had stolen my sense of safety, who had left my family and me scarred in ways the world could never see. But even as my body trembled at the thought, my mind spiraled: How could I face him? How could I stand in a room with the person who had taken so much from me and speak the truth without collapsing? How could I keep the rage from consuming me? How could I stop myself from wanting to make him feel even a fraction of the terror he'd inflicted?

And then the memories came rushing back—the shooting, the chaos, the blood, the screams.

And every night, I had relived it, over and over—every sound, every flash of fear, every unbearable second. And then the robbery in 2018, being held at gunpoint, the world narrowed to the unbearable reality of death inches from my face. My body remembered even when my mind tried to forget.

Yet here I was, alive. Not paralyzed. Not broken. Breathing. Walking. Surviving. And for that, I had to remember Him—Jesus. He had carried me through every shattered moment, every sleepless night, every fear-laden heartbeat. I was alive to watch my children thrive: to see them laugh, play basketball, run in the park, face life with strength I could barely comprehend.

The trial, however, remained elusive. Dates were delayed. Month after month, the offender and his attorney stretched the process, trying to wear me down. I knew their strategy, but that didn't erase the terror that gripped me each time the calendar flipped. I wasn't ready. I wasn't prepared to sit in a courtroom where I would be interrogated as if I were the criminal, where the man who had caused so much chaos would look at me, smug or unmoved.

And yet, every night, in the silence of my room, I could feel Him guiding me. I whispered prayers, sometimes through tears: *"Lord, give me strength. Help me walk through that fire. Do not let me falter. I can't do this without You."*

Then came 2021, and a call that rattled me to my core. A voice from the past, a person I could not name to protect lives, spoke words I had longed to hear: "Yeah, Shay, you know what you're talking about. I overheard two dudes talking and one said—'Yeah, man, my homie f**** up and got the wrong person.'"

Mistaken identity. That was it. That single, devastating truth made my blood run cold. My life, Chico's life, all stolen over a tragic error. But there was nothing I could do—no recording, no evidence, only the echo of a truth too late. I hung up, silent, trembling, my chest tight with frustration and grief.

Then came another moment of divine grace. My 30th birthday took me to Cancun, Mexico. The warm sun, the turquoise water, the palm trees swaying gently in the breeze—it was paradise. For a few days, I could almost forget. But even in that bliss, my heart beat with the ache of absence, the pain of survival, the gnawing truth of what had been stolen. I prayed constantly for my children and my family, asking God to protect them while I was so far away.

Returning home, I felt the weight of decisions pressing against me. I had a good-paying job, but my spirit was restless, searching. On the flight back, I whispered: "Lord, what should I do? Please show me. Give me a sign."

Sleep refused me. Instead, a movie caught my eye: *The Lucky One.* "The smallest thing can change your life. In the blink of an eye, something happens by chance… sets you on a course you never imagined. Sometimes finding the light means passing through the deepest darkness."

Tears streamed down my face. God was speaking. I knew it.

Days later, a dream confirmed it—a vision both terrifying and profound. I was in a backyard, calm, surrounded by people, when a company truck I'd never brought appeared. Suddenly, I was thrown inside. It drove itself, crashing into a garage first and then a gigantic tree. A long pipe then burst out of the ceiling of the truck and from it a golden liquid poured into my mouth. I choked. I gasped. I woke up in a panic, my body trembling, heart hammering.

I fell to my knees, hands open, desperate.

Lord, am I going to die? What do You want me to do? Please, speak!

And then it happened. I felt it immediately: a presence, a force. My hands were open, held tightly yet gently, and a voice—soft, yet commanding—spoke to my soul: "Speak."

It was Him. The Lord Jesus Himself. I felt Him there, in the room, holding me, guiding me, showing me purpose and direction. I cried like I had never cried before, tears streaming, heart breaking open and pouring out pain, trauma, fear, and gratitude all at once.

And then, the unimaginable. My bedroom door slowly opened on its own. I thought it was my son, Eman, coming to comfort me. But no one was there. The door opened gently, deliberately, as if touched by divine hands, and I knew without doubt: the Lord Jesus was in my room.

Movies like *The Lucky One* and *The Book of Eli* suddenly made perfect sense. Logan, Eli—they were led by God's hand, through rubble, chaos, and darkness. They were guided to their purpose, protected along the way.

So was I. So had I always been.

Through dreams, visions, and divine encounters, I came to understand something profound: faith requires courage, obedience, and absolute trust. Even in trauma, even in loss, even when darkness surrounds you, God's hand is always there, guiding, protecting, and leading to light.

And I realized, amid my tears and my trembling soul, that I had gained something no one could ever take: JOY.

The trial would come. Justice would come. But even if it didn't, I had found something eternal. I was guided, protected, and alive—not just surviving, but thriving. My testimony, my scars, my story—they were my weapons, my proof, my platform. And through them, God was using me to touch millions.

Then came another sign. On October 23rd, 2021, a message appeared on Facebook Messenger—from an old neighbor, someone who had witnessed the South Side with me. She confirmed what I had long suspected: "It was mistaken identity."

Though she couldn't appear in court, she offered a recording of her statement. My heart swelled. Answers. Closure. Peace.

I realized then that even through trauma, even through mistakes, even through unimaginable loss, God's hand was present, guiding, protecting, and providing. My life, my purpose, my children, my testimony—they were all gifts, reminders that the Lord Jesus walks with me, even in the darkest nights, even in the deepest valleys, even in the moments that feel unbearable.

Looking back, in that quiet apartment, in the early morning hours, I knew it with absolute certainty: the Lord Jesus was in my room. He was real. He was present. And I would never, ever be alone again.

Chapter 23: Trial's Finally Here & Life After

For six long, agonizing years, I had awaited this day—the day the murder trial would finally begin. February 1, 2022, arrived like a storm on the horizon, and even though I had envisioned it countless times, nothing could have prepared me for the reality of it. I felt numb, paralyzed, and utterly overwhelmed. The night before, sleep didn't come easily. I forced my eyes shut, but my mind replayed the horrors of that day over and over. Now, I would face the coward who had shot me, shot at my babies, and stolen an innocent life. I would stand in the same room as the man who had forced me to witness death itself.

Have you ever seen someone bleed from their nose and mouth, struggle to breathe, and watch the light fade from their eyes? Have you ever heard your child scream in terror, unlike anything you imagined possible, their cries carving into your soul, leaving a permanent burn on your heart? I have. I had to watch my seven-month-old tremble in his car seat, shaking uncontrollably. I had to watch my seven-year-old try to figure out how to survive in the chaos, screaming at the top of her lungs. Every flashback tears me apart to this day. No child should ever have to witness bullets flying toward them. Two innocent children, trapped in a hail of death, is a reality that shatters the human heart.

I prayed that night as I had never prayed before, begging God for the strength to face the offender and his family. Could I walk into that courtroom? Could I hold it together? Would I break down? Could I speak the truth without crumbling? My mind raced with endless questions, but finally, exhaustion claimed me, and I drifted into a deep, prayerful sleep. I needed rest. I needed peace for my troubled mind and shattered soul.

The trial was scheduled for nine a.m., and I arrived at the courthouse alone. Strangely, I didn't want anyone with me. I couldn't bear the comfort of someone else's shoulder. I would be too vulnerable, too human. I needed only one presence beside me: the Lord's. In the parking garage, detectives and officers guided me from my car, ensuring I avoided any chance encounter with the offender's family. No one would accompany me, no friendly faces, no reassuring hand—only the law, my lawyer, and my faith.

The trial didn't actually begin until evening. I spent hours waiting in a closed room, pacing the walls of my mind while officials checked in periodically. Anxiety, fear, and exhaustion churned inside me like a storm. I clutched a photo of my children in my hands, staring at their innocent faces to gather courage. My emotions collided violently—terror, anger, determination, grief, and a strange, bitter readiness all at once. If not for prayer, I might have fainted.

I then remembered what others previously said to me. "Kashe, you survived a bullet in your face. You watched your children and Chico endure horrors no one should endure. You spent agonizing days in the hospital, learning to walk, to feed yourself, to be a mother while broken in every way. You held your children tight even when you weren't sure you could breathe yourself. Kashe, you are strong. Stronger than you know."

They were right. So, I held my head high, shoulders squared, stepping into that courtroom with a calm I didn't feel. The Lord had kept me alive for a purpose, and today, I would honor that purpose. I would show the offender the strength he had awakened in me. I would survive, and I would testify—not just for justice, but for the souls of my children and my family.

Inside the courtroom, my nerves sharpened. The offender sat mere feet away, attempting to avoid my gaze. My heart thudded violently. Should I lash out? Could I speak without breaking? My hand clutched the photograph of my children like a lifeline. With trembling fingers, I placed it in my lap. This was real. He was here. Alive. And I was alive.

"State your name for the record," began the State's Attorney.

Questions followed, such as age, occupation, education, number of children, small, procedural, but each one felt like a test of endurance. The judge's demeanor unnerved me; her calmness, her casual sipping of a soda, made her seem detached from the human tragedy unfolding in her courtroom. She had once been a defense attorney, I later learned. This was her first murder trial. A strange coincidence, or perhaps a reminder that life rarely hands justice on a silver platter.

Then came the pivotal moment.

"Please tell me what happened on February 27th, 2016."

I gripped my children's picture tightly. Tears streaked my face as I recounted every horrifying moment—the laughter in the car, the offender himself rushing up to the car, the sudden eruption of gunfire, the blur of bullets, my children's terror, the smell of blood, the chaos frozen in time, the offender running away and Chico taking his last breath. I described the scene with precision, even as my voice cracked and my heart threatened to break under the weight of memory. The State's Attorney guided me gently, asking about the weather, the time, my children's actions, mines and even Chico's. I answered, each word a testament to survival.

I sat through the prosecutor's recounting of the events—the meticulous setup, the multiple vehicles, the orchestrated violence. Watching the sequence of events play out in the courtroom felt like a slow-motion replay of my worst nightmares. During these sessions, I often caught glimpses of him. He would fidget in his seat, glance around nervously, and occasionally glance at me, but he would never make eye contact with me. I could feel the hatred and contempt I carried in my gaze, even when I tried to mask it. He had once wielded power over my life, and now the tables had turned. I had survived, I had endured, and he was powerless to harm us any longer.

Then it was the defense attorney's turn. His tone was sharp, confrontational. "What were you doing as the bullets flew?" "Describe the offender at the time." "You only saw him briefly?" I held my ground, answering honestly, refusing to be intimidated. I relived the horror, but I endured, and I endured for my children, for Chico, and for myself.

The defense attorney attempted to diminish my testimony, questioning every detail of what I had seen, heard, and felt. "Are you sure you saw him clearly?" he asked. "Can you truly identify him?" I felt a surge of anger rise within me. I took a deep breath, stood taller, and recounted every detail with precision—the way he moved, the cold calculation in his eyes, the hair, the hoodie, the gun. I described the fear that had gripped my children and me, the adrenaline that kept me alive, the memory that no legal argument could erase. My voice trembled, but my words were unwavering. I was a survivor. I was a witness. I was a mother demanding justice.

When closing statements came, the defense argued I was desperate to point fingers, that I had misremembered details, and that my recollection was flawed. I shook my head internally. I remembered him—the hooded figure, the thick hair beneath the hoodie, the tall, imposing stance. I remembered the alley, the sound of bullets, the faces of my children frozen in terror. Cognitive recall isn't perfect, but trauma imprints itself with ruthless accuracy. I had survived, and I had seen.

The verdict arrived by Zoom on February 3rd. My heart sank when I heard the words: "Not guilty." The offender would walk free. Despite every detail I provided, despite the camera that did catch the whole ordeal that went down like I said it did…justice was denied in the eyes of the court. Since the camera couldn't pick up his face or license plates, my eyes weren't good enough. My soul fractured, and I fell into a depression that rivaled the day I had been shot. For weeks, I moved through life like a ghost. Bills remained, responsibilities persisted, but I felt dead inside. The mental and emotional pain cut deeper than the three bullets that had once ripped through my body.

Yet, even in despair, I knew God's plan remained. The offender's release was not the end, it was a chapter in a larger story. I could not understand it, but I could trust it. I could grieve, I could feel the loss, and I could continue to fight for my children, my family, and my own healing.

I had survived bullets, trauma, and grief. I had witnessed death and endured emotional devastation. And I would survive this, too. I would rise, again, and again, because life—and God—demanded it.

Chapter 24: Revelation, Waking Up for Good

The start of 2022 was heavy. I was still healing from heartbreaks that stemmed from situations I had placed myself in, compounded by the aftermath of the trial and all the chaos that had consumed my life. Bills piled up, rent was late, and I struggled to maintain even the basics for my kids. We stayed in a two-bedroom apartment—small, but it was home, however temporary it felt. Life was tolerable at best, but God was showing me glimpses of what He had in store, and I couldn't yet reach the visions He whispered to me about. Most days, I felt like a failure.

Being a single mother after losing Chico was hard beyond measure. Every birthday, every milestone, I watched my children grow without their father by their side. Anyone who has experienced this understands the ache. I am grateful for my life and my kids, but there were moments when the weight of it all threatened to crush me. Most of their friends had both parents cheering them on at birthday parties and sports events. For us, it was just me, tired, stretched thin, constantly balancing care and survival.

And truthfully, I wasn't always the mother I wanted to be. My patience frayed. My children—being children—tested boundaries, pushed limits, and sometimes clashed with me. In my exhaustion, I resorted to yelling when I should have spoken calmly. I tried to compensate for the absence of a father figure, and in that attempt, I often failed. I didn't physically harm my children, but I realized that instilling fear instead of respect created barriers between us. It led to moments of tension, shutdowns, and miscommunication. Slowly, I made the conscious decision to change that— to let them have a voice, to foster an environment of understanding, patience, and unity.

On top of parenting struggles, I had long-standing personal issues to address. My insecurities, my shyness, my naivete—they all stemmed from the absence of my biological father. That absence left a massive hole in my heart, one I tried to fill with attention, validation, and experiences that ultimately drained me. Recovery was ongoing, but I wasn't fully walking in the light—I was still too accustomed to the dark.

By mid-2022, I had fallen behind on rent, car payments, and bills. I stayed in my apartment as long as I could, trying to catch up and reclaim some sense of normalcy, but it didn't work. The apartment management wasn't flexible, and I eventually had to move in with my sister and mom, rotating homes to survive. While they were gracious, I felt lost without my own space. Every day I posted on social media, helping others stay strong in their storms, all while keeping my personal struggles hidden. I didn't lie, but I masked my pain, presenting strength to the world even when I felt like falling apart.

Yet, God's hand was present even in the darkness. He provided when I had nothing, comforted me during lonely nights, and reminded me to pray, fast, obey, and thank Him daily. By the end of the year, I began to notice profound shifts within myself. I was filled with the Holy Spirit, a sensation so marvelous it left me in awe. I joined a church community, released emotionally toxic relationships, and began speaking publicly again—interviews with *The Power Hour* and *The Washington Post* marked milestones in reclaiming my voice. My children and I were baptized together for the first time on October 2nd, 2022, a spiritual rebirth that symbolized our shared healing and newfound faith.

I began fasting and praying earnestly for the first time, witnessing miracles in ways that left me speechless. I even forgave the shooter—the one who had taken Chico, endangered my children, and nearly ended my life. Forgiveness felt impossible for years, but the Holy Spirit guided me to release that pain. I forgave not for him, but for me—for my children, for my own soul. Carrying that burden would have destroyed me. God's forgiveness taught me to let go, to reclaim peace that no human or circumstance could take from me.

Another monumental step was reconnecting with my biological father. Yes, Paul will forever by my father and we still have a great relationship today, but I had to open and close this chapter. For years, I had only one memory of him, a fleeting phone call in childhood. After tracing family members online, speaking to a cousin, and eventually messaging my half-sister, I slowly opened a door I thought long sealed. Initial obstacles arose—miscommunication, fear, and family dynamics—but I prayed, waited, and remained patient.

Finally, in December 2022, I walked into his nursing home. The moment he asked, "Are you, my daughter?

Are you, Kashe?" tears flowed freely. That single acknowledgment, that one hug, and those three words— "I love you"—delivered closure I had been seeking for decades. Even though he was sick, even though his mind was compromised by years of mental health struggles, we were able to speak, forgive, and reconcile in a way that felt complete. My children later met him and witnessed the lineage and history I had longed to share with them.

Through 2022, I faced hardship, disappointment, and pain, yet I also experienced profound spiritual growth. I learned the power of forgiveness, the strength in patience, and the necessity of walking in God's light. I began to understand that all my trials—childhood trauma, the shooting, single motherhood, familial estrangement—were shaping me, testing my faith, and preparing me for the life He had planned.

Entering 2023, I felt a renewed sense of purpose. I was not where I wanted to be, but I trusted God's plan. I had surrendered my life fully to Him, and for the first time, I could breathe without the weight of resentment, fear, or anger constricting my chest. I was awake mentally, spiritually, and emotionally, and ready to embrace the next chapter of my life.

I realized that life's storms are inevitable, but through faith, forgiveness, and obedience, we can rise above. We can heal. We can breathe. And we can trust that God's promises are true: "For I know the thoughts I think toward you, says the Lord, thoughts of peace and not of evil, to give you a future and a hope" (Jeremiah 29:11, NKJV).

Today, I urge anyone reading this to let go of grudges, forgive freely, and treasure the people in your life who are genuine. Hold on to joy, celebrate the small victories, and trust that even in your darkest moments, God is orchestrating miracles. Life is not perfect, but it is beautiful—and with faith, we can navigate it with peace.

As writer Marisa Donnelly expressed in *Thought Catalog*, "He gave us miracles and blessings, stories and strangers to find us when we needed them the most."[2] I believe that wholeheartedly. And so here I am, sharing my story, hoping it reaches someone's heart, and testifying that no matter the storm, we will be just fine.

Chapter 25: WHY?

"Why?" The question that haunted me for years. The question everyone wanted answered. The one that echoed in my mind every night, in every prayer, in every tear shed for Chico, for my children, and for myself.

And now, finally, the truth emerged.

It all came down to mistaken identity. That's why Chico was hurt, confused, and lost after his death. He hadn't done anything to deserve it. He didn't understand what had happened, and neither did we. I remember his words from our spiritual encounter, still vivid in my mind: "I don't know, Kashe... I just don't know!"

He couldn't accept that he was gone. He didn't comprehend the finality of death or the injustice that had stolen his life. All the 'what ifs' I had tortured myself with over the years suddenly made sense, offering a faint measure of solace. Still, nothing could erase the horror of the day we shouldn't have had to experience at all. God, however, in His divine wisdom, sent three people to help us piece together the truth we desperately needed.

Even as clarity arrived, I was confronted with lingering danger. Threats on social media reminded me that the world could be cruel, vindictive, and unforgiving—even when you are innocent. Yet, knowing the truth brought me closer to peace, and that peace allowed me to tell the story fully and without hesitation.

1. **The Associate:**

The first confirmation came from an associate who lived in the area. Just hours after the shooting, he posted publicly:

> **Facebook Post, February 27th, 5:13 PM:**
> "R.I.P. to my n***** Chico from Bucktown. He wasn't even from where you thought he was. It's cool. (2 gun emojis) Fired. I will find out. Love you, cuz my n*****. See you when I get there. We're gonna talk about how we turned up for New Year's. This picture, b*** a** n***** I swear, it's cracking."

Every detail he wrote confirmed what my heart had feared and yet longed to know—the shooting wasn't personal, it wasn't revenge, it wasn't a misunderstanding in the traditional sense. It was chaos, random in its execution, cruel in its consequence. Chico's death wasn't meant for him, but it happened.

2. **The Local Shop Witness:**

The second confirmation came via a personal phone call.

> **Phone Call Transcript**:
> Ring, Ring, Ring
> Me: Hello?
> Person: Yeah, Shay, you know what you're talking about, fo sho.
> Me: What are you talking about?
> Person: I'm sitting here kicking it at a shop, overhearing two dudes talking. One said, "Yeah, man, my homie f***** up and got the wrong person."
> Me: Wait… are they talking about Chico? Are you serious?
> Person: Yes… I can't say too much. People are coming in and out. I just

heard it… and watched. It's messed up, man.

Me: Thank you. I'll call you back.

Hanging up, I sat in disbelief. My mind reeled—how could something so devastating, so final, happen because of a mistake? The realization was bitter, but clarity is a gift, no matter how painful.

3. **The Neighbor:**

The third confirmation came from a neighbor we had known years before. Her name remains private for her safety.

> **Facebook Messenger:**
> "Hi Kashe, I was your neighbor across the street—the one who always smiled and said 'hey neighbors.' My daughter is 11 now. I praise God for your strength. I know and believe every bullet you took was protecting your children. Call me, I'd like to tell you something."

I hesitated at first, wary of scams or setups. But God reminded me: *Trust, Kashe. Just call.*

The neighbor confirmed what the others had told me: one of the local men admitted, "This was all mistaken identity." Chico's death had been a tragic accident. Nothing he did provoked the attack; it was a cruel twist of fate. She offered to leave a voice recording for the court to validate what she had witnessed and heard. Her courage, her willingness to help despite risk, was a gift. She reminded me that even in the darkest places, God sends people to speak truth.

> **Neighbor's Voice Recording Excerpt:**
> "I am aware I am being recorded and consent. I am an old neighbor of Kashe and Eric's. I saw their story online and reached out. One of the older guys from the block said it was mistaken identity. They came back thinking Eric was someone else from the day before."

Three separate sources, three separate confirmations. The pattern was undeniable. God's truth had arrived.

4. Threats on Social Media:

Even as truth unfolded, darkness lingered online. On September 5, 2021, while hosting a TikTok live titled "What's Your Purpose? strangers appeared, defending the shooter, making threats, and referencing my children.

Comments Captured:
- baochenchen32: "Free ******"
- baochenchen32: "The babies didn't get hit tho."
- ajshottayasiin: "A gang should pull up and take turns on you."

The brazenness of these strangers reminded me that evil often lingers, even when the truth is known. But even in these moments, I held onto faith. God is the ultimate judge. He is the final arbiter. Despite man's failures, His justice is perfect.

Closing Reflections:

Yes, the judge allowed the offender to walk free. No, nothing could be used in court, such as the recordings or social media threats. No, none of the potential witnesses wanted to come to court out of fear. Yes,

Chico died for no reason other than being in the wrong place at the wrong time.

Yes, there was a video, but as it showed how it all went down, unfortunately it wasn't able to clearly show his face. Yes, my children and I endured trauma no one should ever endure. Yes, my life is not easy. But God—

BUT GOD was always there. He guided, protected, and strengthened us. He orchestrated every detail, sent us confirmations, and helped us forgive what could have broken us forever.

I write this not for revenge, not for blame, but for clarity. To show that even when the world fails, even when justice falters, God's plan remains intact. My mission in sharing this story is not anger—it is revelation, closure, and the power of faith.

Chico's life, though tragically cut short, now serves as a testimony. His death was senseless, yet through it, God's presence became unmistakable. My children learned resilience. I learned forgiveness. And we all learned that truth, even in the darkest hours, has the power to heal.

This story is a testament to the human spirit, the power of prayer, and the miracles God works through unseen hands. Every source, every voice, every confirmation was a gift—a reminder that God's truth prevails even when human courts fail.

To those reading: hold your loved ones close, pray without ceasing, forgive fiercely, and trust God's timing. Even in tragedy, life's lessons are profound, and the strength to rise above is always available when we place faith over fear.

Life will test you. Fate may strike without reason. But faith, perseverance, and forgiveness are your ultimate weapons. What was taken from us cannot erase what we build from the ashes. This is why I share my story—to inspire resilience, hope, and trust in God's plan.

Chico's death was a tragedy, but through God, it became a catalyst for healing, revelation, and awakening. This is the truth I carry forward. And it is my prayer that anyone reading this finds their strength, their voice, and their peace—no matter the storms they face.

Because in the end, the question of **"Why?"** finds its answer not in human understanding, but in the infinite wisdom of God.

Final Reflection: Lessons from Loss and Victory

"For I know the thoughts I think toward you, says the Lord, thoughts of peace and not of evil, to give you a future and a hope."
– Jeremiah 29:11, NKJV

What I Learned Through My Journey:

1. Faith Is Stronger Than Fear
Life may take unexpected turns, and tragedy may strike, but faith in God anchors the soul. Even when courts fail, even when others don't see the truth, God's justice and love prevail.

2. Forgiveness Sets You Free
Forgiving those who have wronged you is not about excusing their actions—it's about freeing yourself from carrying the weight of anger, pain, and resentment. Forgiveness heals the heart and restores peace.

3. Truth Is Your Shield

In a world that may judge, twist, or deny reality, holding onto your truth protects you. Be honest, stand firm, and let God's light guide you through dark circumstances.

4. Closure Comes From Within

You cannot always control others, but you *can* reclaim your peace. Seek answers, understand your story, and allow God to guide your healing.

5. Purpose Arises From Pain

Even in the midst of loss, betrayal, or fear, your experiences can fuel a mission. Use your journey to help others, to teach, and to shine a light in dark places.

My Pledge to Life:

- To live boldly, even after heartbreak
- To guide my children with love, faith, and integrity
- To honor Chico's life by transforming pain into purpose
- To stand for truth, justice, and the power of God's plan
- To rise above fear, threats, and adversity with courage

A Final Word:

Why did this happen? Why did I lose so much? Why did tragedy strike when life seemed fragile?

I may never fully understand the depth of human cruelty, but I know this: God had a plan. My children and I are alive, our voices are heard, and our story—though filled with pain—stands as a testament to resilience, faith, and ultimate victory.

The final verdict is not in the courts. It is in the Lord. And His verdict is always justice. Always love. Always redemption.

Rise. Heal. Forgive. Believe. Live.

Message to My Readers

I wish I could say I understand exactly how you feel—but grief is deeply personal. What I can say is that I know the kind of pain that comes when violence steals someone you love. It leaves questions, anger, and a silence that feels unbearable.

If you are reading this with a shattered heart, please hear me: you are not weak for hurting. You are not faithless for questioning. And you are not alone—even when it feels that way.

There were moments when I didn't think I would survive the weight of my loss. Moments when breathing felt like work. Moments when God felt far away. Yet somehow, He was still there—holding me together when I couldn't hold myself.

You don't have to rush healing. You don't have to be strong all the time. Take one breath. One step. One prayer at a time. God sees every tear, and none of this pain is wasted. Your loved one mattered. Your pain matters. And your story is not over.

No matter the trials, tribulations, devastation, or disappointments you face, I urge you to choose courage. Choose to keep going even when the weight feels unbearable, and the path ahead is unclear. There will be moments when life tests your faith, stretches your endurance, and challenges everything you thought you knew about yourself. In those moments, remember this: your struggle does not define your ending.

God never promised the journey would be easy, but He did promise that we would never walk it alone. When your strength is gone, His remains. When hope feels distant, He draws nearer. Every tear you shed, every silent prayer you whisper, and every step you take in faith matters more than you realize.

Obstacles are not proof of defeat; they are often evidence of growth. Even in pain, God is working, shaping, refining, and preparing you for what lies ahead. What feels like a delay may be protection. What feels like loss may be making room for something greater.

So, hold on. Take the next step, even if it's a small one. Trust that God's presence surrounds you, carries you, and sustains you through every season. Your story is still unfolding, and there is purpose in your perseverance. What's ahead is worth the fight, and you are never, ever alone.

With love and understanding, *Kashe*

References

1. Brow, Les. Quotes by Les Brown [Quotes page]. Goodreads. https://www.goodreads.com/author/quotes/57803.Les_Brown
2. Donnelly, Marisa. "Miracles, Blessings, and Unexpected Encounters." *Thought Catalog*, 2020.

Faith Stronger Than Bullets: A Grief & Healing Study Guide

For readers navigating loss, trauma, and the long road toward hope.

How to Use This Study Guide:

This guide is designed to walk alongside you as you process grief—especially grief caused by sudden or violent loss. You may use it individually, with a trusted friend, or in a small group. Move at your own pace. There is no timetable for grief.

Each section includes:
- A key Scripture
- A reflection grounded in faith and lived experience
- Guided questions for journaling or discussion
- A prayer
- Practical steps for the week

You are invited to be honest, gentle with yourself, and open to God's presence in every stage.

Section 1: When the Shock Is Still Fresh

Scripture:

"The Lord is close to the brokenhearted and saves those who are crushed in spirit." —Psalm 34:18, NIV

Reflection:

Grief often begins with shock. Your body and mind may still be trying to make sense of what happened. Numbness, confusion, anger, or silence are not signs of weak faith—they are human responses to deep loss. God does not wait for you to have the right words. He draws near when your spirit feels crushed.

Reflection Questions:

- What emotions feel closest to the surface right now?
- In what ways does your body carry your grief?
- What does it mean to you that God is *close* even when nothing feels okay?

Prayer:

Lord, I don't know how to carry this pain. I feel broken and overwhelmed. Draw near to me in this moment. Hold what I cannot. Amen.

Practical Step:

Give yourself permission to rest. Limit decisions this week. Grief is work.

Section 2: Asking "Why?" Without Shame

Scripture:

"Trust in the Lord with all your heart and lean not on your own understanding." —Proverbs 3:5, NIV

Reflection:

Violent loss often brings questions that feel unanswerable. Why them? Why now? Why this way? God is not threatened by your questions. Faith does not require silence—it invites honesty. Trust does not mean understanding everything; it means choosing to lean when answers are incomplete.

Reflection Questions
- What questions have you been afraid to say out loud?
- How has unanswered grief affected your faith?
- What might it look like to bring your questions directly to God?

Prayer:

God, I don't understand what happened. I am trying to trust You while my heart aches with questions. Meet me in the middle of my doubt. Amen.

Practical Step:

Write a letter to God saying everything you wish you could say without censoring yourself.

Section 3: Grief and Anger Can Coexist with Faith

Scripture:

"In your anger do not sin." —Ephesians 4:26, NIV

Reflection:

Anger after loss—especially violent loss—is common. Anger at circumstances, systems, people, even God. Scripture acknowledges anger without condemning it. What matters is where we take it. God invites us to bring our anger to Him rather than letting it consume us.

Reflection Questions:

- What makes you angry about this loss?
- Have you allowed yourself to feel that anger honestly?

- How might expressing anger safely help your healing?

Prayer:

God, I am angry, and I don't know what to do with it. Teach me how to release this without letting it harden my heart. Amen.

Practical Step:

Channel anger through movement—walking, stretching, or creative expression.

Section 4: When Faith Feels Fragile

Scripture:

"We live by faith, not by sight." —2 Corinthians 5:7, NIV

Reflection:

There may be days when faith feels distant or weak. This does not mean God has left you. Faith in grief is often quieter, slower, and less certain—but still real. God honors even the smallest steps toward Him.

Reflection Questions:
- How has your faith changed since your loss?
- What feels hardest to believe right now?
- What small act of faith feels possible today?

Prayer:

Lord, my faith feels fragile. Carry me when I cannot carry belief on my own. Amen.

Practical Step:

Read one verse a day. Let that be enough.

Section 5: Carrying Love Forward

Scripture:

"Love never fails." — Corinthians 13:8, NIV

Reflection:

Grief is love with nowhere to go. Though your loved one is no longer physically present, love does not disappear. God can help you find ways to honor that love—through memory, legacy, and compassion.

Reflection Questions:
- What did your loved one teach you about love?
- How do you want their life to be remembered?

- What would it look like to carry their love forward?

Prayer:

God, help me honor the love I still carry. Teach me how to live in a way that reflects the gift they were to me. Amen.

Practical Step:

Create a small ritual of remembrance—lighting a candle, journaling, or prayer.

Section 6: Hope After Trauma

Scripture:

"He heals the brokenhearted and binds up their wounds." —Psalm 147:3, NIV

Reflection:

Healing does not mean forgetting. It means learning how to live again while carrying scars with grace. God binds wounds slowly and tenderly. Progress may feel uneven—but it is still progress.

Reflection Questions:
- What does healing mean to you right now?
- What fears do you have about moving forward?

- Where do you see even the smallest signs of hope?

Prayer:

Healer of my heart, bind what is broken within me. Restore me in Your time and Your way. Amen.

Practical Step:

Seek support—a counselor, pastor, or trusted community member.

Final Encouragement:

Scripture:

"'For I know the plans I have for you,' declares the Lord… 'plans to give you hope and a future.'" — Jeremiah 29:11, NIV

Even after unimaginable loss, God is still writing your story. Hope may look different now—but it is still possible.

(The following page may be repeated or placed after each section as desired.)

Prayer & Reflection Page

Use the space below to write prayers, questions, or reflections as you continue your healing journey.

Date: _____

Reflection Title: _____

Prayer:

_____

_____

_____

_____

_____

_____

Date: _____

Reflection Title: _____

Prayer:

_____

_____

_____

_____

_____

_____

Leader's Guide: Walking With Others Through Grief

Purpose of This Guide:

This leader's guide is designed to help pastors, counselors, small-group leaders, and trusted facilitators walk alongside individuals who are grieving sudden or violent loss. Faith Stronger Than Bullets is not a quick-fix study. It is a sacred space.

Your role is not to solve grief—but to hold space, point consistently to Christ, and model compassion.

Suggested Format:

Length: 6–8 weeks

Group Size: 3–8 participants recommended

Session Length: 60–90 minutes

Materials Needed: Bibles, journals, tissues, quiet atmosphere

Leader Posture & Guidelines:
- Lead with listening, not lecturing
- Do not pressure participants to share
- Avoid platitudes or theological shortcuts
- Allow silence—it is sacred

- If trauma surfaces beyond your capacity, gently encourage professional support

Weekly Session Flow (Suggested):
- Opening prayer (short and gentle)
- Scripture reading (aloud)
- Brief reflection from the study guide
- Open-ended discussion questions
- Journaling or quiet reflection time
- Closing prayer or blessing

Discussion Prompts for Leaders:
- What emotions surfaced this week?
- Where did you sense God's nearness—or absence?
- What feels hardest to release right now?
- What does courage look like this week?

Special Note on Violent Loss:

Grief caused by violence often includes anger, fear, and confusion. Affirm these emotions without judgment. Remind participants that Jesus Himself grieved violently and unjustly at the cross.

Closing the Study:

End the final session with a blessing, candle lighting, or prayer of release.

Healing is ongoing. This study is a beginning—not an ending.

Leader's Prayer:

Lord, help me walk gently. Help me listen well. Help me love as You love those who are brokenhearted. Amen.

Further Resources

<u>Memory, Cognition, and Trauma Recovery</u>:

- Clemente, Dr. M. *Cognitive Techniques to Improve Memory Recall.* Journal of Psychological Research, 2018.
- "Closing Your Eyes Boosts Memory Recall, New Study Finds." *ScienceDaily*, 16 January 2015, https://www.sciencedaily.com/releases/2015/01/150116085606.htm
- Gough, Myles. "Closing Your Eyes Helps You Remember More Accurately." *ScienceAlert*, 16 January 2015, https://www.sciencealert.com/closing-your-eyes-helps-you-remember-more-accurately
- Messer, Erica. "Criminal Minds: Evolution | The Science Behind Cognitive Interviews." Paramount+ YouTube Channel, 2023, https://www.youtube.com/watch?v=Uah51ZngNS0&t=2s, Accessed 25 March 2023.

Spiritual Growth, Faith, and Healing:
- Donnelly, Marisa. "Miracles, Blessings, and Unexpected Encounters." *Thought Catalog*, 2020.
- Lucado, Max. *Anxious for Nothing: Finding Calm in a Chaotic World.* Thomas Nelson, 2017.
- *The Holy Bible*, New King James Version. Thomas Nelson, Inc., 1982.
- Wright, N.T. *Simply Jesus: A New Vision of Who He Was, What He Did, and Why He Matters.* HarperOne, 2011.

Personal Resilience & Life Transformation:
- Brown, Brené. *Rising Strong: How the Ability to Reset Transforms the Way We Live, Love, Parent, and Lead.* Spiegel & Grau, 2015.
- Dweck, Carol S. *Mindset: The New Psychology of Success.* Ballantine Books, 2006.
- Sinek, Simon. *Start With Why: How Great Leaders Inspire Everyone to Take Action.* Portfolio, 2009.

Legal & Justice System Insights:
- Friedman, Lawrence M. *Crime and Punishment in American History.* Basic Books, 1993.
- Innocence Project. *Understanding Eyewitness Misidentification,* https://www.innocenceproject.org/eyewitness-identification
- Loftus, Elizabeth F. *Eyewitness Testimony.* Harvard University Press, 1979.

Acknowledgments

It has taken many years for this book to come to life. When I first began writing it, I was still very young and carrying the weight of more than most people ever see. I had endured trials, heartbreak, and deep loss—and being shot felt like the final blow. Yet even then, writing remained my refuge. It carried me to places of peace when my reality felt overwhelming, allowing me to breathe when life pressed in too hard.

One day, I realized that God had entrusted me with these experiences—not to bury them, but to share them. Every setback I survived revealed how faithfully He was working in me, shaping, teaching, and molding me into the woman I am today. I am far from perfect, but I am committed to growing, healing, and doing better each day.

I questioned this book many times. I knew it would reach far beyond me, and that responsibility felt heavy. But God walked with me through every doubt, every delay, and every revision. My purpose is simple: to tell the truth. Without Him and without the countless people whose names appear in these pages, this testimony would not exist.

I wanted this book released immediately, but God had other plans. He required more time, more wisdom, and deeper understanding so that His love and glory could be shared with integrity and intention. I now trust His timing completely.

I dedicate this book to Chico. May you continue to soar. The Lord confirmed to me that you made it home and received your beautiful wings. You are deeply loved and forever missed.

I also extend my deepest gratitude to Dr. Sinha and his beautiful wife, Mrs. Sinha, Ms. Trisha, the team at Oral & Maxillofacial Surgery of Chicago, Advocate Christ Medical Center, and the angels who worked tirelessly within those walls. To the Burns family—thank you for helping raise my babies while I worked and pursued my education. To my family and friends, and most of all to the Lord Jesus Christ, who entrusted me with this powerful testimony—thank You.

And to my children—Kaniya, Jeremiah, and Eman—you are my heart. You taught me patience, kindness, and unconditional love. I did not fully understand true love until I became your mother, and I did not fully understand it until I sought my Heavenly Father. Because of that, I can now teach you about Him and His promises. You gave me strength when I left the hospital and chose to keep going. Your hugs, your love, and your resilience carried me. Without you, there is no me. God placed us together for a purpose—to fulfill our assignment. I love you beyond words, and there is nothing I would not do for you—even take bullets.

Kashe is a survivor, devoted mother, and woman of unwavering faith whose life was forever altered by a senseless act of violence. In broad daylight, she survived a gun attack that claimed the life of her partner and left her critically wounded in front of her children—an experience that shattered her sense of safety and reshaped every part of her life. What followed was not only a fight for physical survival but a profound spiritual and emotional journey through grief, trauma, and unanswered questions.

In the aftermath of loss and injustice, Kashe leaned into her faith as both a lifeline and a source of strength. Through prayer, perseverance, and a deep reliance on God, she began the long and often painful process of healing—learning how to live again while carrying grief, raising her children, and confronting a justice system that failed to provide closure. Her testimony is one of courage in the face of fear and hope that refuses to be extinguished. In her memoir, *Faith Stronger Than Bullets*, Kashe courageously shares her story to offer comfort and encouragement to others navigating loss, trauma, and injustice. With honesty and compassion, she invites readers into the reality of surviving what should have destroyed her and discovering that God's presence remains steadfast even when life feels broken beyond repair.

Kashe's story is a powerful reminder that while tragedy can alter a life in an instant, faith—rooted in God's love and promises—can rise stronger than fear, pain, and unanswered questions. Through her voice, she seeks to inspire others to hold onto hope, trust God in the darkest moments, and believe that healing, though not linear, is possible.

www.ingramcontent.com/pod-product-compliance
Lightning Source LLC
LaVergne TN
LVHW040143080526
838202LV00042B/3008